Ray Simpson lives on [illegible] ...dian of the Community of Aidan and Hilda which facilitates a fresh cradling of Christian spirituality through soul friendship, retreats and provision of resources for individuals and churches.

He is an Anglican priest and was commissioned by Free and Roman Catholic Churches and the Society of Friends (Quakers), to pioneer an ecumenical project.

He is the author of *Give Yourself a Holy Island Retreat*, *Celtic Worship Through the Year* and a number of other books on Celtic spirituality.

Other books by the same author

Give Yourself a Holy Island Retreat (St Aidan Press, The Open Gate, Holy Island)

Celtic Blessings (Hodder & Stoughton, UK; Loyola Press, USA)

Celtic Worship Through the Year (Hodder & Stoughton)

Before We Say Goodbye (HarperCollins)

Soul Friendship (Hodder & Stoughton)

Exploring Celtic Spirituality (Hodder & Stoughton)

A Holy Island Prayer Book

Morning, Midday and Evening Prayer

Ray Simpson

**Illustrations by
Denise Adam**

Morehouse Publishing
NEW YORK · HARRISBURG · DENVER

*I dedicate this book
to the people of Holy Island.*

Text © 2002 in this compilation by Ray Simpson

First North American Edition 2003
Morehouse Publishing, 4775 Linglestown Road, Harrisburg, PA 17112
Morehouse Publishing, 445 Fifth Avenue, New York, NY 10016

Morehouse Publishing is an imprint of Church Publishing Incorporated.

First published in 2002 by the Canterbury Press Norwich (a publishing inprint
of Hymns Ancient & Modern Limited, a registered charity), St. Mary's Works,
St. Mary's Plain, Norwich, Norfolk, NR3 3BH, UK

Typeset by Regent Typesetting

Library of Congress Cataloging-in-Publication Data
A holy island prayer book : morning, midday and evening prayer / (compiled
by) Ray Simpson. – 1st North American ed.
      p. cm.
   Includes bibliographical references
   ISBN 0-8192-1935-5 (alk. paper)
   1. Prayers. I. Simpson, Ray.
BV245.H58 2003
242'.8—dc21   2002141411

Contents

Introduction

Holy Island is the birthplace of the Lindisfarne Gospels, that literary crown of the medieval golden age. In 1958 Queen Elizabeth was presented with a book of Holy Island pilgrim meditations whose illuminated inscription was inspired by these Gospels. The inscription assured Her Majesty of prayers that her realm would 'continue to profit from the example of spiritual power shown forth through the ages by one of its least yet greatest parts – Lindisfarne, the Holy Island which inspired this book.'

'One of its least yet greatest parts' – that is the secret of the best spirituality. It is in the ordinary, everyday things of life, and in the little things of creation that we find the presence of God and are renewed day by day. It is in our weakness that we are strong. It is that spirit, please God, which breathes through these prayers.

From Lindisfarne, Christianity was taken to English-speaking people by the seventh-century mission spear-headed by Aidan of Ireland, the 'people's saint', gentle of heart, determined as steel. Since English-speakers now cover the world as the waters cover the sea (eighty per cent of the material on the worldwide web is in English), this story and the prayers inspired by Aidan's island deserve to be widely known.

Morning and Evening Prayer and Holy Communion have long been offered each day of the year at Holy Island's St Mary's Church. These form a stable monastic-style framework. In addition, pilgrims from

Introduction

many lands pray in informal and creative ways at the island's three churches, on the beaches, while walking the Pilgrims' Way, and in hotels and centres. The prayers for morning, midday and evening in this book reflect this variety.

After David Adam (the author of many books on Celtic spirituality) became vicar, a theme for each day of the week was introduced into St Mary's daily services. These themes draw from time-honoured Jewish and Christian tradition and are followed in this book, as set out on the Contents page. The days of the week are grouped together for five weeks, and a reflection introduces each of the seven days' themes. Each midday prayer also has a short reflection based on a geographical feature of the island.

The book may be used as a daily prayer book, once, twice or three times each day in a monthly cycle, or it may be used as an occasional resource to dip into. However this book is used, I hope it makes both earth and heaven more real to you.

Ray Simpson
The Holy Island of Lindisfarne
Epiphanytide 2002

Sunday

New Life

*Statue of St Aidan with the castle
in the background*

Sunday: *New Life*

New Life is the theme of our Sunday prayers because it is the first day of the week, when Jesus Christ, Son of the Living God, rose from the dead. The Christian Faith is about nature, individuals and communities dying and rising again in Christ.

Jesus rose from the dead on the first day of the Jewish week. That week was based on the sabbath, reflecting the belief that God created the world in six days and then rested on the sabbath. For Christians, therefore, Jesus' resurrection on the day after the sabbath became 'the eighth day', the beginning of a new creation, the inauguration of a time of special purpose which would culminate in the return of Christ to complete the transformation of the universe.

Early Christians, such as John on Patmos Island (Revelation 1:10), spoke of the first day of the week as 'the Lord's Day'. The fourth-century founder of a Christian community at Edessa explained that Christians gathered together on the first day of the week 'because on that day Christ rose from the dead, and it will be again on that day that he will appear to us at the end.' That is why some Christians turn to face east (where Christ rose from the dead and whence he will come again) when they say the Christian creeds.

Sunday is also a day of light. In the pagan Roman Empire the first day of the week was known as Sun's Day. In the second century Justin, the great Christian teacher and martyr, explained to the Emperor

Sunday: *New Life*

Constantine that Christians met on this day because it was on Sun's Day that Jesus appeared to his friends after his death. Constantine was a worshipper of 'the Unconquered Sun', which he believed to be the protector of his empire, but he also had a vision of the Cross of Christ in the sky. He decreed that Sunday should be a special day of rest and recreation for soldiers and law officers.

The linking of Christ with the sun comes from biblical, early Christian and Celtic insights and is at the heart of Holy Island spirituality. The Old Testament prophet Malachi referred to the coming Messiah as 'the sun of justice who would rise with healing in his rays' (Malachi 4:2). A third-century mosaic at St Peter's Necropolis, Rome, depicts Christ as Helios, the sun god, driving his chariot into heaven. The Lindisfarne monks may have told the story of St Patrick lighting the Easter fire in Ireland to celebrate the rising from death of Christ, whom he called 'the true Sun'.

Early in the morning of 1 January 2000 the road from the harbour to the castle on Holy Island was crowded with visitors looking east, waiting for the sun's rising. Among them was a lady dying of cancer. She explained, 'I was determined to live long enough to see the sun rise on Holy Island on the first day of the millennium.' That morning the sun leapt across the sea to bathe us in glory.

Lindisfarne is an island of light, for the sea all around it reflects back and magnifies the sun's light. On this island we see every sunrise as a sacrament. The island is also a parable of decay and new life, death and resurrection. For although there have been periods of invasion, pillage and neglect, there have also been periods of renewal and resurrection. To celebrate the third millennium of Christ, pilgrims and members of

4

Sunday: *New Life*

all of Holy Island's churches took part in a fifty-event festival entitled 'Saints Uprising'.

The light still shines in the darkness. The life of Christ is always stronger than death.

Sunday: *New Life*

Week 1: Morning

Rejoice all spirits!
The ascending sun shines alike on the living and the
dead.
As the true Helios, Christ climbed the heights of
heaven.
Christ the Sun of suns, risen from the wintry ground
of death,
now scatters the darkness from our path.
Rejoice, O earth, in shining splendour,
Radiant in the brightness of your King!
Christ has conquered death! Glory fills you!
Darkness vanishes for ever! Alleluia!
Exult in glory! The risen Saviour shines upon you!
Alleluia!

God, renew me
from the crown of my head to the soles of my feet.
Amen.

Psalm 81
John 11:17–27

The glorious gold-bright sun was rising on the crests of
the great hills, and it was changing colour – green, pur-
ple, red, blood-red, intense white, and gold-white, like
the glory of the God of the elements to the children of
men. It was dancing up and down in exultation at the
joyous resurrection of the beloved Saviour of victory.

Carmina Gadelica[1]

Sunday: *New Life*

Risen Christ we welcome you.
You are the flowering bough of creation;
From you cascades music like a million stars,
Truth to cleanse a myriad souls.
From you flee demons, omens and all ill will;
Around you rejoice the angels of light.

The Community of Aidan and Hilda

Christ of the Easter rising
Hope is one of your best gifts to us
So teach us to give it to others.

A prayer from Brazil

*

Week 1: Midday reflection
at St Cuthbert's Centre

Lindisfarne was described as 'the holiest place in England' by Alcuin, Advisor to Charlemagne, the Holy Roman Emperor. A king of England decreed that it should be officially known as Holy Island because so many pilgrims thronged to its shrine of St Cuthbert. In recent years St Cuthbert's United Reformed Church has been transformed into an attractive Visitors' Centre. Those who complete the sixty-mile St Cuthbert's Way walk from Melrose to Lindisfarne officially finish it there, sitting outside on a specially sculptured seat which includes a representation of St Cuthbert's staff in wrought iron.

Lindisfarne has also been called Cradle Island, for here Christianity was cradled for the English-speaking people, and is still being cradled. Pilgrims and tourists visit it to find the peace of God or spiritual direction for their lives.

A friend of mine decided to ride on horseback across the sands with the woman he loved, go down on his knees in the churchyard, propose marriage to her and then return to the mainland. The proposal went to plan, but when the time came to make the return journey, they found that the tide had turned. 'Don't worry, the horses can swim,' they were told. As they returned through the rising waters their elation was mixed with terror.

This is an island full of proposals – God's proposals. So can our lives be. But be warned: the excitement of clinching something with God is often followed by immersion in the waters of difficulty.

Job 19:23–27

Dear Father God
I have voyaged to this place and here I pause.
My life so far has brought me here.
My future stretches farther than the eye can see.
If thus far my journey you have shared, accompany
    me now.
Give wisdom, light, and always joy
so that in my thought and gift and love
my life shall be to fellow travellers
a witness to your presence in the world.
Amen.

Ian Fosten[2]

*

Sunday: *New Life*

Week 1: Evening

This night, O Victor over death:
Raise me from the death of denial
Raise me from the death of fear
Raise me from the death of despair.

This night, O Victor over death:
Wake me to the eternal 'Yes'
Wake me to the rays of Hope
Wake me to the light of Dawn.

Psalm 30
John 20:1–10

Risen Christ, watch over us this night
And keep us in the light of your presence.
May our praise continually blend
With the song of all creation.

Great God, as you brought Christ
safely through the night of sin and death
to his rising at dawn
so bring us through this night
that we may offer you our lives afresh at dawn.

*

Week 2: Morning

I arise today through the strength of Christ's birth
and baptism.
I arise today through the strength of Christ's
crucifixion and burial.

Sunday: *New Life*

I arise today through the strength of his resurrection
  and ascension.

I arise today in the brightness of sun
I arise today in the splendour of fire
I arise today in the speed of lightning.

Based on St Patrick's Breastplate

Psalm 33
2 Corinthians 4:13–18

Gratitude for the sun: blinding pulsing light
through trunks of trees, through mists, through walls
warming caves and corridors
– he who wakes us –
in our minds so be it.

Based on a Mohawk prayer

Life of Jesus, Sun of suns, filling every part of us
Life be in our speech
Sense in what we say
The bloom of cherries on our lips
Till you come back again.

Love of Jesus, Sun of suns, filling every heart for us
Give us love in what we do
Filling us for everyone.
Traversing sea and road and field
Rays of Jesus be our shield.

Based on an early Celtic prayer

May this be a day of resurrection and refreshment
  for families and single people, for traders and
  communities.

Sunday: *New Life*

May our homes be places of hospitality and hope,
   that we may know your risen presence as we share
   ourselves
   and enjoy the company of others.
May our churches worship in a way that brings
   honour to you,
   joy to the people, and healing to the land.

*

Week 2: Midday reflection
on the Heugh

From the Heugh, the hill between the priory and the
shore, one can look across to Bamburgh and beyond
towards the Lammermuir Hills.

At Bamburgh Aidan died, some say of a broken
heart, for the Christ-like king who had made possible
Aidan's mission had been cruelly killed in battle, and
perhaps Aidan feared that his life's work had been a
failure.

That night was black, yet stars shone brightly. In the
Lammermuir Hills a young man keeping sheep
sat bolt upright. The sky was alive with light and
movement. Were they shooting stars? Or were those
lights, shaped like angels, bearing a holy soul to glory?

The young man was Cuthbert. Next day he learned
that the holy soul being borne aloft was Aidan of
Lindisfarne. He decided he would leave behind his
silken clothes, his horse and servant and sword, and
offer himself to God's service for the rest of his life.

Thus from despair came hope; from death came life.
Under Cuthbert's leadership the mission would go
from strength to strength. That pattern can be ours too
– for it is in dying that we live.

Sunday: *New Life*

2 Corinthians 4:7–12

Renew us, O Risen Christ, in the midst of the day.
In doubt bring faith
In disillusion bring hope
In indifference bring mercy
In expediency bring ideals
In the staleness of routine bring stirrings of life.

*

Week 2: Evening

We lie down in peace knowing our sins are forgiven;
We lie down in peace knowing death has no fear.
We lie down in peace knowing no powers can harm
    us;
We lie down in peace knowing angels are near.

Psalm 118:15–24
John 20:11–18

Risen Christ of the apostles,
Bring renewal to the church,
to ordained ministries and religious orders.
Raise up new callings and communities
which meet the need of our times.

Risen Christ of the scars,
who spoke peace to your desolate disciples,
Speak peace this night to your desolate ones.

Risen Christ of the lake-side,
who nourished and inspired your disciples,
Inspire us and our loved ones to rest this night in
your presence.

Sunday: *New Life*

The eye of the Risen Christ be upon us as we sleep
The eye of affection and mercy
The eye of joy and gladness
Bringing to dawn our wholeness.

*

Week 3: Morning

Shine on us, Lord, like the sun that lights up day.
Chase away the dark and all shadow of sin.
As day follows night
May we be bathed in your glory.

Psalm 66
Isaiah 11:6–9

Christ Jesus, in the light of your risen presence,
and in union with your first frail apostles, we say
    sorry:
For not weighing your words,
For not sharing your trials,
For not believing your promises.

O loving Christ, hanged on a tree yet risen in the
    morning,
Scatter the sin from our souls as the mist from the
    hills.

Based on a prayer from Iona Abbey

Those whose faces are turned always towards the
    sun's rising
See the living light on its path approaching,

Sunday: *New Life*

As over the glittering sea where in tide's rising and
  falling
The sea beasts bask, on the Isles of Farne.
Aidan and Cuthbert saw God's feet walking
Each day towards all who on world's shores await
  his coming.
That we too, hand in hand, have received the
  unending morning.

Kathleen Raine

The God of life go with us
The Risen Christ beside us
The vibrant Spirit within us.

*

Week 3: Midday reflection
at Cuddies Beach

Each year Northern Cross pilgrims walk many miles,
each group carrying a large wooden cross, and on
Good Friday, in bare feet, they cross the sands by the
pilgrim posts. The next day Roman Catholics,
Anglicans and others gather for vigil in St Mary's
Church and then walk in darkness to Cuddies Beach
(the beach in front of Cuthbert's Isle). There a fire is lit,
as once the risen Christ lit a fire by Galilee's shore, and
the Easter candle, symbolizing the risen Christ, Light of
the world, is lit from the fire. The song that follows the
reading below is sung and the crowd returns to share
Holy Communion in the church.

Sunday: *New Life*

John 21:15–25

Christ as a light illumine and guide me
Christ as a shield overshadow me
Christ under me
Christ over me
Christ beside me on my left and my right
This day be within and without me
Lonely and meek yet all powerful
Be in the mouth of each to whom I speak
In the mouth of each who speaks to me
Christ as a light illumine and guide me.

John Michael Talbot[3]

*

Week 3: Evening

Spirit of the Risen Christ,
As the lamps light up the evening,
Shine into our hearts and kindle in us the fire of
 your love.

Psalm 126
1 Peter 3:18, 22

This is the night when you saved our forebears
delivering the people of Israel from their slavery
and leading them dry-shod through the sea.
This is the night when Jesus Christ vanquished hell
 and rose triumphant from the grave.
This is the night when all who believe in him are
 freed from sin
 and restored to grace and holiness.

Sunday: *New Life*

Most blest of nights, when wickedness is put to flight
    and sin is washed away,
lost innocence is regained and mourning turned to joy.
Night truly blessed, when heaven is wedded to earth
and all creation reconciled to God!
Grant that this Easter candle may make our darkness
    light
For Christ the Morning Star has risen
and is alive and reigns for ever and ever. Amen.

From the Easter Eve Vigil

Risen Christ, you have entered into darkness, despair
    and death
Rising in glory, you accompany all who have to enter
    into these
You give us the cup of life
You quench our every thirst
You turn hearts of stone into flesh
You clothe the peacemakers in raiment of light
Live in us now and bring us to our resurrection
    without end.

*

Week 4: Morning

Rising from death, today Christ greets his people
Rising with all creation, we greet him as our King.

Glory to you Christ our King
Radiant with light
The Sun who shines on all the world.
Earth exalt!
Heaven rejoice!
Morning and night give thanks and praise!

Sunday: *New Life*

Psalm 136:1–3, 23–26
1 Corinthians 15:1–8

St Cuthbert on Holy Island

When last the raging spring storm had abated
And the night's dark banners from the East had fled;
He swiftly rose, and donned his simple raiment
And barefoot left behind his narrow bed.

Heedless of thorn and stone, he sought the seashore
And on a rock he sat and watched the sun
Rise in the East flooding resurrection.
A gull called out, a new day had begun.

Across the calming waters sang the sea-hounds,
Mothers calling for their snowy young
A shoal of fish swam near the rock he sat on
Spinning, spinning silver in the sun.

And one by one he watched the world renewing –
A cricket chirped, a bee sought out a flower.
He picked a shell strewn careless on the shoreline
And marvelled at the Architect's great power.

The sand, each grain, lay perfect in arrangement
To leave the imprint of his searching feet,
Refreshed and calm he retraced his journey
And Oh! the upward climb seemed hard yet sweet.

Who knows this man, what words he used in praying
Or what his soul had seen beyond the sea.
Perhaps he was out fishing with his Master
Or busy storing sweetness like the bee?

L. Smith[4]

Sunday: *New Life*

Come to us in our pilgrimage of life
And bring us to our place of resurrection.

*

Week 4: Midday reflection at St Mary's Church

It is thought this church is on the site of the very first wooden church built by Aidan. The little rounded arch high in the main arch between the pulpit and the organ is thought to go back to Saxon times. If so, it is earlier than the ruins of the Benedictine Priory outside.

There is a great deal to see in this ancient and beautiful building, including a facsimile copy of the Lindisfarne Gospels, and carpets in front of the two altars. These are beautifully worked copies of two pages from those Gospels, handmade by women of the island.

The Lindisfarne Gospels were written and illuminated in Lindisfarne's monastery scriptorium in about 724. They contain 258 pages of calf skin sized about 34 by 26 centimetres. They are a prized exhibit in the British Library, London, as well as in digital form at Lindisfarne's Heritage Centre. Yet it was once thought that this treasure was lost for ever.

The monks were taking it to Ireland for safe keeping during Viking invasions in 875 when it was washed overboard in a storm. Simeon of Durham recounts, however, that the monks were divinely inspired to stop off at Whithorn monastery, where someone found it washed up at a very low tide. The colours were intact, nothing was even blurred. They took this as divine guidance that they should not, after all, emigrate to Ireland. It was a kind of resurrection.

Sunday: *New Life*

Exodus 31:1–11

In you, O Christ
Light is stronger than darkness
Good is stronger than evil
Trust is stronger than greed
Wisdom is stronger than ignorance
Life is stronger than death.

Desmond Tutu (adapted)

*

Week 4: Evening

Into our place of darkness
Into our place of strife
Into our fears and worries
Come with your risen life.

Into those who are dying
Into those weary of life
Into those tired from exertions
Come with your risen life.

Psalm 118:1–14
Luke 24:13–32

Risen Christ
You burned in the hearts of two walkers
 who made room in their converse for you.
Burn in us as we converse.

You revealed yourself to them as they welcomed you
 into their home.

Sunday: *New Life*

Reveal yourself to us as we make a welcome in our
homes.

You fell asleep in mortal flesh, O Lord and Leader,
But on the third day you rose again.
Now you watch over us as we sleep,
You restore our souls and preserve our life.
In love of you we will take our rest.

*

Week 5: Morning

Arise, shine, for the rays of God's glory touch the
earth
The Sun of suns is rising
Kings and peoples shall be drawn to the light.

I welcome the light that burns in the rising sun
I welcome the light that dawns through the Son of
God
I welcome the light that gleams through the growing
earth
I welcome the light that shines through saints and
signs
I welcome the light you kindle in my soul.

Psalm 5
1 Thessalonians 5:4–11

The tender shoot bursts into sight
The light floods dark lands
Drooping hearts rejoice
And the people say Amen.

The lame leap for joy
Blind eyes, closed ears are opened

Sunday: *New Life*

All people see God's splendour
And the people say Amen.

Glory to the Birther
Glory to the Son
Glory to the Spirit
Ever Three in One.

*

Week 5: Midday reflection at Mo Jowett's seat

Mo Jowett's seat backs onto the old lighthouse on the Heugh and commemorates a young mother whose life was tragically cut short. Carved on the bench are these words: 'Mo Jowett 1951–99. One who left the city's crowds to find a place of solitude to seek God only face to face . . . .'

However busy we are, it is necessary to create times of solitude and contemplation. Through solitude we reconnect with hidden springs of life. Through contemplation we become aware once again of the Divine Presence in our midst.

Isaiah 40:27–31

Jesus –
Truly God, truly human
Truly infinite, truly frail
Your greatness holds the universe
Your lovely countenance attracts our hearts
Your goodness beckons all that is good in us
Your wisdom searches us

Sunday: *New Life*

Your truth sheds light on our darkness
Your generosity enriches our poverty
Your friendship consoles the unwanted
Your strength turns away all evils
Your justice deters wrong-doing
Your power conquers hell
Your love-enflamed heart kindles our cold hearts
Your miraculous hand fills us with all blessings
Your sweet and holy name rejoices all who love you
Your mercy brings forgiveness.
Have mercy on us
Give us eternal life
For your glory fills eternity;
Your glory fills the universe.

*

Week 5: Evening

Light of the world, in grace and beauty.
Transparent flame of love's free duty
    You bring salvation to our race.
Now, as we see the lights of evening
We raise our voice in hymns of praise
    Worthy are you of endless blessing
    Sun of our night, lamp of our days.

Traditional

We offer to you, Lord, the troubles of this day;
we lay down our burdens at your feet.
    Forgive us our sins, give us your peace,
    and help us to receive your Word.
In the name of Christ. Amen.

23

Sunday: *New Life*

Psalm 117
John 20:19–23

We give you thanks, our Father, that you are always present, in all things, each day and each night. We give you thanks for your gifts of creation, life and friendship. We give you thanks for the particular blessings of this day . . . .

Into your hands we place our families, our neighbours, our brothers and sisters in Christ, and all whom we have met today; enfold them in your love.

Into your hands we place all who are victims of prejudice, oppression or neglect; the frail, the unwanted . . . . May everyone be cherished from conception to the grave.

Into your hands we place all who are restless, sick, or prey to the powers of evil; keep guard over them and keep them from harm.

May you be
lit by the glory of God
drawn by the light of God
warmed by the fire of God.

Brian Frost

Monday

Creation

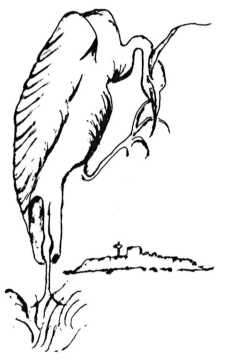

St Cuthbert's Island in the distance

Monday: *Creation*

In Jewish tradition, as we have seen, the first day of the week reflects the first day of creation. Since Christianity uses Sunday to celebrate Christ's rising from death, we use Monday, the first day of our working week, to focus on creation. Human beings are co-creators with God; therefore on this day we celebrate and pray for the world of human work and creativity as well as the world of nature.

Secure in its Jewish roots, the early church set the human drama of good and evil in the context of a creation in which God delights (Genesis 1:31). Creation is groaning to be made complete, and is on tiptoe to see God's children bring it into a deeper relationship with God (Romans 8:19). God has called us to be the first fruits of this creation (James 1:18).

The ninth-century Irish teacher, John Scotus Eriugena, in his book *The Division of Nature*, echoed the teaching of John's Gospel (John 1:1) that God is the 'Life Force' within all things, and concluded that therefore 'every visible and invisible creature can be called a theophany.'[5] We seek daily to see in the visible things of creation the eternal things of God (Romans 1:20).

In 1854 the US Government offered to buy a large area of Indian land and promised a 'reservation' for the Indian people. This reply, attributed to Chief Seattle, is a beautiful and profound statement on the environment:

Monday: *Creation*

We are part of the earth and it is part of us. The perfumed flowers are our sisters; the deer, the horse, the great eagle, these are our brothers. The rocky crests, the juices in the meadows, the body heat of the pony, and human beings – all belong to the same family.

The rivers are our brothers – they quench our thirst. The rivers carry our canoes, and feed our children. If we sell you our land, you must remember, and teach your children, that the rivers are our brothers, and yours, and you must henceforth give the rivers the kindness you would give any brother.

The white man treats his mother, the earth, and his brother, the sky, as things to be bought, plundered, sold like sheep or bright beads. His appetite will devour the earth and leave behind only a desert.

There is no quiet place in the white man's cities, no place to hear the unfurling of leaves in the spring, or the rustle of an insect's wings.

This we know: all things are connected. Man did not weave the web of life; he is merely a strand in it. Whatever he does to the web, he does to himself.

You may think that you own God as you wish to own our land; but you cannot. He is the God of all human beings, and his compassion is equal for the red and the white people. This earth is precious to him, and to harm the earth is to heap contempt on its Creator.

Chief Seattle

When we misuse the creation, God permits the creation to punish us. Columbanus taught that 'Those who trample on creation trample on themselves.' Our prayers provide for confession for our misuse of creation, but above all they express wonder.

Monday: *Creation*

You never enjoy the world aright, till the sea itself
floweth in your veins, till you are clothed with the
heavens, and crowned with the stars, and perceive
yourself to be the sole heir of the whole world.

Thomas Traherne[6]

Week 1: Morning

I arise today in the goodness of creation
I arise today in the verdure of the fertile ground
I arise today in the promise of the rising seed

Psalm 19
Genesis 1:24–31a

Glad Bringer of brightness
Day's blessing, rainbow's embrace
Teach our hearts to open as the buds open
And to welcome in your grace.
Teach us to dance with the playful clouds
And to laugh with sun's smile on our face.
The earth is yours, may it bring forth its produce
The birds are yours, may they bring forth their songs
Our work is yours, may it bring forth its yield.

O Son of God, change my heart.
Your Spirit composes the songs of the birds
    and the buzz of the bees.
Your creation is a million wondrous miracles,
    beautiful to look upon.
I ask of you just one more miracle:
    beautify my soul.

*

Week 1: Midday reflection
on Cuthbert's Isle

When I first came to live on Holy Island I heard a sound
that was strange to me – the cry of the seals. 'Are they in

childbirth?' I asked David Adam, the vicar. 'They're praising God,' he replied. I began to listen more thoughtfully to the sounds of God in creation. In summer common seals lie on the sandbanks of Cuthbert's Isle, and grey seals inhabit the rocks at the other end of the island.

We can listen to the sounds of creation whether we are on islands or on the mainland, for, as my London landlady once said to me, 'People are my scenery.' God pulses through engines, computers and people as well as through beasts. Some urban pilgrims to Holy Island fear that this is not so. I encourage them to do what Columba did – to make God their island as they return to their towns and cities.

Lord, you are my island
In your bosom I nest.
You are the calm of the sea
In that peace I rest.
You are the waves on the shore's glistening stones
Their sound is my hymn.
You are the song of the birds
Their tune I sing.
You are the sea breaking on rock
I praise you with the swell.
You are the ocean that laps my being
In you I dwell.

Attributed to Columba

Job 38:1–15

I will go forth to sow my seeds
And every seed that lies
Beneath cold winter's eyes
Shall take root in God's way.
Kissed by the winds that lightly run
The new blades shall leap to greet the sun.

Monday: *Creation*

May the blessing of the earth be on us
the great round earth.
May we ever have a kindly greeting
for people we pass on our way.
And now may the Lord bless us and bless us kindly.

An old Irish blessing

*

Week 1: Evening

In the womb of darkness all life is conceived
The blackness of space gave stars their birth
From a star's death was born our earth
Out of earth's buried depths were born our
    mountains and valleys.

Nature's breath and eyes are clearest blue
O purest God, gaze on us this night.
The blackbird's call is wild and free
Rejoicing at the new abundance of food.
May our spirits become free this night
Rejoicing in your abundance.

Psalm 148
Isaiah 45:3–8

We wait in the darkness expectantly, longingly.
Only in the darkness may we see the splendour of the
    universe
and the glowing stars.
It was in the darkness the wise three saw the star that
    led them
to the Christ-child.

33

Monday: *Creation*

In the darkness of sleep dreams rise up.
In the darkness God gave dreams to Joseph and the
wise three.
With you, Creator God, there is treasure in the
darkness.

Peace to the land and all that grows on it
Peace to the sea and all that swims in it
Peace to the air and all that flies through it
Peace to the night and all who sleep in it.

*

Week 2: Morning

God of life, you summon the day to dawn
And call us to create with you.
You are the Rock from which all earth is fashioned
You are the Food from which all souls are fed
You are the Force from which all power lines travel
You are the Source who is creation's head.

Psalm 104:24–30
Colossians 1:9–20

You made the earth and through the long ages
planted it with every kind of plant.
You made animals to crawl and to run upon it,
birds to fly over it, and fish to swim around it.
When all was prepared, you formed humankind
from the soil,
You breathed your life into them.
You made the sun to shine upon them all.
Spilled on this earth are all the joys of heaven.

Based on a North American Indian liturgy

34

Monday: *Creation*

God bless the earth that is beneath us
The sky that is above us
The day that lies before us
Your image deep within us.

*

Week 2: Midday reflection at the incoming tide

Lindisfarne is a tidal island. Its rhythm beats with the tides.

For with the flow and ebb, its style
varies from continent to isle;
Dry-shod, o'er sands, twice every day,
the pilgrims to the shrine find way;
Twice every day the waves efface
of staves and sandall'd feet the trace.

Sir Walter Scott

The Creator has built rhythm into creation. We are rhythmic creatures, in our breathing, walking, waking, sleeping and in our progression through the seasons of life. Do we embrace this rhythm or run from it?

Mark 4:26–28

Ebb tide, full tide
Let life's rhythms flow
Full tide, ebb tide
How life's beat must go.

David Adam

*

Week 2: Evening

Lindisfarne Rhythm

Ebb tide, full tide, praise the Lord of land and sea.

Barren rocks, darting birds, praise God's holy name!

Poor folk, ruling folk, praise the Lord of land and sea.

Pilgrimed sands, sea-shelled strands, praise God's holy name!

Fierce lions, gentle lambs, praise the Lord of land and sea.

Noble women, mission priests, praise God's holy name!

Chanting boys, slaves set free, praise the Lord of land and sea.

Old and young and all the land, praise God's holy name!

The Community of Aidan and Hilda

Psalm 104:1, 10–24
Joel 2:21–27

After creation God rested
We give back our lives to you
Thank you for your love for us, strong and nurturing
We give back our lives to you
Thank you for our minds and bodies
We give back our lives to you
Thank you for the past day
We give back our lives to you.

You created the world out of love;
Now we return to you in love.
We will rest in you this night
And awake in newness of life.

*

Week 3: Morning

Glorious Source, we give you greeting!
Let Sister Earth and Brother Sun praise you,
Let the fields and the forests praise you,
Let the birds and the beasts praise you,
Let everything that has breath praise you,
Mother and Father of all that has being.

Psalm 124
Matthew 6:25–33

Dear Saviour, who restored unity between earth and
    heaven,
        teach us to care for your earth,
and to be good stewards of all that is in it.
May our eyes be open to see your hand in nature.
May our hands be open to cherish your gifts
    in the material things around.
May we learn how to live in harmony with your
    laws.
Bless the soil on which we live and work
    and make community.
May it bring forth goodness
    to nourish and renew all who share it.

May the road rise to meet us
May the wind be at our back
May the sun shine on our labours
May the soft rains fall on our fields of endeavour.

Ancient Irish (adapted)

*

Week 3: Midday reflection
at two gardens

There are two very different gardens on Holy Island. The first is the walled garden built by Gertrude Jekyll to satisfy her gaze when she was in residence at the castle during July and August. This is dominated by large clumps of summer-blooming flowers that catch the eye when viewed from the castle.

The second is the monastic garden strip that borders St Mary's Church. This contains plants which were grown in Britain during the period of St Cuthbert. It is part of the Sacred Land Project. Photo displays of these plants have been produced. They include a prayer by David Adam which begins: 'O God of beauty and grace, open our eyes to the beauty around us. Let us see in leaf and flower, in bud and shrub, signs of your glory and tokens of your love.'

Genesis 49:22–26

Life-giver
Bring buds to flower
Bring rain to the earth
Bring songs to our hearts.

Renewer
May gardens become green
May beauty emerge
May dreams come to pass.

*

Week 3: Evening

We bless you, Lord
For the beauty of the trees
The softness of the air
The fragrance of the grass

We bless you, Lord
For the soaring of the skies
The rhythms of the earth
The stillness of the night

We bless you, Lord
For the freshness of the morning
The dewdrops on the flower
For the twinkling of the stars

We bless you, Lord
For the taste of good food
The trail of the sun
And the life that never goes away

Chief Dan George

Psalm 16
Romans 1:18–21

Creator and Saviour, we have:
exploited earth for our selfish ends
turned our backs on the cycles of life
and forgotten we are your stewards.
Now soils become barren
air and water become unclean
species disappear
and humans are diminished.
In penitence we come to you.

Monday: *Creation*

In dependence on the God of life
May we cherish the precious earth,
The earth of the God of life
The earth of the Christ of love
The earth of the Spirit Holy.
In dependence on the God of life
May the earth be our bed of hope.

*

Week 4: Morning

The sun rises daily only because you command it
Its splendour will not last, created things all perish
Christ the true Sun nothing can destroy
He shall reign for ever.

Psalm 67
Exodus 23:14–19

This we know, the earth does not belong to us
The earth is God's and so are all people
This we know, we did not weave the web of life
The earth is God's and so is all that breathes on it
Whatever befalls the earth
    befalls the sons and daughters of the earth
The earth is God's and so we will serve it.

May the blessing of the rain be on us, the sweet soft
    rain.
May it fall upon our spirits
so that all the little flowers may spring up
and shed their sweetness on the air.
May the blessing of the great rains be upon us
that they beat upon our spirits

and wash them fair and clean
and leave there many a shining pool
where the blue of heaven shines, and sometimes a star.

*

Week 4: Midday reflection on the dunes

One mid-summer's night, the late John Collins, a Holy Island naturalist, sensing that this might be the last time he could do such a thing, led us on a nature walk over the dunes. We placed a sheet under a tree, shook the tree, and counted by torch-light the myriad living things that had fallen onto the sheet. We listened to the night birds. We traced the first hints of dawn in the sky. Next day we were more aware of the mystery and wonder of the little things in nature, and of the elements in creation which seem to echo characteristics that the Creator has planted in our own souls.

May I be real, like the elements
May I be true, like the fire
May I be free, like the wind
May the love that is within me flow, like water.
And may I not forget the fifth element, the flowers.
Dear God, give me fragrance in my relationships.

John 6:26–35

Great Spirit, whose breath is felt in the soft breeze,
We seek your strength at noon.
May we, and the peoples of the world
Work in dignity and walk in the beauty of the day.

*

Week 4: Evening

Let the light fade and the work be done
Let the flowers and the desk-tops close
Let the sun go down and the world become still
And let the Son of God draw near.

Psalm 104:1–4
Luke 12:4–7

For the rainforests gone,
    and the deserts caused by human destruction
We grieve with you, O God.
For polluted seas, and dirty streets
We grieve with you, O God.
For not being content
    to savour the simple gifts of creation
We grieve with you, O God.

As the sun circles the world
Circle this land, O God.
Circle the soil, circle the waters
Circle the crops, circle the homes
Keep harm without, keep good within.

*

Week 5: Morning

Creator, you caused the earth to bring forth the
    Saviour
Spirit, come now and renew the face of the earth
All that grows on it, all who live on it.

42

Monday: *Creation*

We give you thanks
Because earth's life and fruitfulness flow from you
And all times and seasons reflect your laws.
We give you thanks
Because you created the world in love
You redeemed the world through love
You maintain the world by your love.
Help us to give our love to you.

Psalm 50:1–15
Job 38:22–41

We believe, O God of all gods
That you are the eternal Maker of life.
We believe, O God of all gods
That you are the eternal Maker of love.
We believe, O Lord and God of all people
That you are the Creator of the high heavens
That you are the Creator of the skies above
That you are the Creator of the oceans below.
We believe, O Lord and God of all people
That you are the One who created our souls
    and set their course
That you are the One who created our bodies from
    earth
That you gave to our bodies their breath
    and to our souls their possession.

God, bless to us our bodies
God, bless to us our souls
God, bless to us our living
God, bless to us our goals.

*

Week 5: Midday reflection
at the bird hide

The bird hide, which overlooks a lake on the path between the castle and the white Emmanuel Head beacon, sometimes has a list of birds that recent visitors have spotted. It is said that some 158 species have been seen on the island. There at the bird hide you can sit, observe and ponder.

Birds teach us about the world of the Spirit. Which wild places does the Spirit wish you to fly into? In what ways are you trying to cage God's Spirit?

Catch the Bird of Heaven . . .
Bell and book and candle cannot hold him any more
Still the Bird is flying, as he did before.
Ah, the Bird of Heaven! Follow where the Bird has gone
If you want to find him, keep on travelling on.

Sidney Carter

Luke 12:22–31

Caring Father, in you we live and move and have our being. Provide for those who can neither sow nor reap because human ills have drained them of energy or motivation.

Give us wisdom to manage technology for the world's good. Sustain those who eke out minerals, create textiles, grow crops or rear cattle.

Bless all work done today that enables the human family to be clothed, fed and housed; to travel and learn wisely, to communicate and exchange, to craft and celebrate, in everything reflecting your glory.

*

Week 5: Evening

Blest be all creation
And all that has life
Blest be the earth
May it uplift our bed tonight
Blest be the fire
May it glow in us tonight
Blest be the water
May it bathe our being tonight
Blest be the air
May it make our night breath sweet.

Psalm 13
Philippians 4:4–9

Earth-maker God, as the hand is made for holding
    and the eye for seeing
You have fashioned me for joy.
Grant me your vision that I may find it everywhere –
In the sunlit faces of our world
In the wild flower's beauty, in the lark's melody
In a child's smile, in a mother's love,
In the face of a steadfast man.
Our society is ever restless
Always craving one more thing to do,
Seeking happiness through more and more
    possessions.
Teach us to be at peace with what we have

45

Monday: *Creation*

To embrace what we have given and received
To know that enough is enough
Until our strivings cease
And we rest content in you alone.

Now we give you thanks for work completed
Now we lie down in peace.

Tuesday

Peace

A swan guards the pilgrims way

Tuesday: *Peace*

The peace for which we pray is not just the absence of war. In Bible times God's people were called to strive for the ideal of *shalom* – a caring, fruitful community in harmony with its neighbours, its land and its God. To this God calls us still.

War is the price of the selfishness of nations. We reap what we sow. Human self-will is in itself a form of war against fellow creatures and the Creator. What Christians call the Incarnation – God taking flesh as a human being – is God's way of making peace with us. Celtic Christians picture the Incarnation of Christ as God bounding down a mountainside, reaching out a hand of reconciliation to us. So our prayers and readings for Tuesdays are about the birth of Christ, who reaches out to make us one with God and each other, and to heal the wounds of history.

In the Celtic imagination Bethlehem becomes present in each locality, and our own hearts and homes can become like the stable where Christ was born. I think of Holy Island as the Bethlehem of Britain, an ordinary place where animals, innkeepers, shepherds, visitors and angels all get a look in, and where Christ can still be cradled.

This bare island is more deserted at Christmas than at any other time. It can seem as if nothing is here. But my belief is that it is precisely in the emptiness of that dark womb that fresh life from God can be born. So it can be in the apparently barren and deserted places in our lives.

Tuesday: *Peace*

At his birth Jesus was described as the Prince of Peace. Before his death he said to his disciples, 'My peace I give to you, but my peace is not of this world' (John 14:27). The peace for which we pray is the peace above all peace, the peace of the Son of Peace who reconciles those who are hostile towards each other and towards God.

As the second millennium drew to a close some Christians began to identify wrongs that others felt Christians had committed against them, and to make acts of atoning service. In that way, some of the baggage of hates, hurts, fears and mistrust of the second millennium would not be carried over into the third.

As pilgrims from Roman, Anglican, Reformed and New Church traditions gathered at Lindisfarne in 1997 during their pilgrimage from Rome to Iona, a confession in the following vein was made:

> We confess with shame
> the loss in the church of integrity, humility and patience
> the crushing of spontaneity
> the caging of the wild Spirit
> the breaking off of relationships
> the bruising of the crushed reeds
> the arrogance of the intellect
> the pride of empire-building.
> We accept our share of responsibility for these sins,
> and seek to shed them on behalf of ourselves and our churches.
> Lord, have mercy upon us and forgive us.

In the spirit of that occasion let us ask God to open our eyes to these wrongs, and to touch our hearts with true sorrow. For this is the path to peace.

Tuesday: *Peace*

We swear by peace and love to stand
Heart to heart and hand in hand
Mark, O Spirit, and hear us now
Confirming this our Sacred Vow.

Week 1: Morning

Child of glory, Child of Mary,
 born in the stable, King of all,
You came to our wasteland, in our place suffered.
By choosing to be born as a child
You teach us to reverence every human life.
May we never despise, degrade or destroy it.
Rather, help us sustain and preserve it.

Psalm 8
John 1:1–14

I can always tell when I am completely relaxed to the
Divine Plan by the inner peace that comes to me. This
inner peace brings a joyous, creative urge that leads me
into activities that unfold the Plan, or it brings a
patience and a stillness that allow others to unfold the
Plan to me.

Glenn Clark

The shape of Christ be within us, the shape of Christ
 before us,
The shape of Christ behind us, on Sunday and on
 Monday.
The shape of Christ be over us, the shape of Christ be
 under us,
The shape of Christ around us, on Tuesday and on
 Wednesday.
The shape of Christ be within us, before us, behind
 us,

Within us, around us, on Thursday, Friday and
  Saturday.
Alleluia, alleluia, alleluia, alleluia.

Carmina Gadelica

*

Week 1: Midday reflection
at the stables

Several places on Holy Island used to be stables, since
until the present causeway was built horses were the
main means of transport to and from the island. At the
time of writing the Stables Coffee Bar, in Marygate,
marks the site of one such stable. I once entered another
former stable on the island at midnight on New Year's
night. In the pitch darkness God spoke to me about a
new cradling of Faith as earthy, godly and uncluttered
as the cradling at Bethlehem and the cradling in Aidan's
time.

> It is this ability to fuse together the unique time and
> place of Christ's birth in Bethlehem with our own
> specific present . . . which is part of the genius of
> Celtic spirituality; a realisation that the eternal
> moments of the Incarnation or the Crucifixion or the
> Resurrection can transcend time and space, enabling
> us to relocate Bethlehem or Calvary or the Garden of
> the Third Day in our own back yard.

Patrick Thomas

Matthew 1:18–23

Tuesday: *Peace*

Merciful God, you brought peace into the world not through men of power but on a woman's lap. As we look into the face of the babe of Bethlehem, the face of Defenceless Love, look upon your troubled world. Fear and violence, homelessness and pollution, grief and anxiety stalk it.

Move the hearts of governments and peoples to use your gifts of wealth and skill to build your kingdom of love, where we shall live free from cruelty, neglect and fear, free to look into the face of every person with welcome.

> You are among us, Lord,
>> as you were in the homeless babe in the stable.
> As we come face to face with eternal Goodness,
>> may the human spirit be renewed.

George Appleton (adapted)[7]

*

Week 1: Evening

Christ who comes with justice and peace,
We pray for victims of oppression and violence.
At your birth you were proclaimed the Prince of Peace.
You came to remove the wall that divides one people from another.
May walls of hostility and fear come tumbling down.
You call the peacemakers blest.
Strengthen peacemakers in places torn apart by the ravages of sin.

Psalm 46
Matthew 11:28–29

Tuesday: *Peace*

To come into your presence
You Virgin of the lowly
To come into your presence
You mother of Jesus Christ.

To come into your presence
You dwelling of meekness
To come into your presence
You home of peace.

Carmina Gadelica

May Heaven's peace-keepers encircle us all
    with their outstretched arms
To protect us from the hostile powers,
To put balm into our dreams,
To give us contented, sweet repose.

*

Week 2: Morning

Dear Son of Mary, you took flesh to redeem us,
    change our hearts.
Dear Son of God, you came to us with sacrificial love,
    change our hearts.

The Son of God bounds towards us
    reaching out a hand of reconciliation.
Let us take it, and listen to God's Word.

Psalm 1
Luke 1:26–38

Christ, like us, was made of frail human flesh, in order
to expel sin from human flesh. He came to invite us to

Tuesday: *Peace*

become like himself, commissioning us to imitate God, placing us under obedience to the Father so that we might see and know God. He who did this is the Word of God, who lived in and became Son of humankind in order to accustom humans to live in God and to accustom God to live in humanity. That is why he is a sign of our salvation, Immanuel, born of the Virgin, a sign given us personally by the Lord.

Irenaeus[8]

May the eternal Glory shine upon us
May the Son of Mary stay beside us
May the life-giving Spirit live within us
Now and always.

*

Week 2: Midday reflection at Sandham Bay

The first Viking invasion of Britain was at Lindisfarne in 793. The invaders probably landed at Sandham Bay. The monastery was ransacked, older monks were killed and young ones were taken to Norway as slaves. A carving which depicts this invasion may been seen in the Priory Museum.

That invasion was ghastly, but it was not the last word. Those young slaves brought the life-changing peace of Christ to their owners' households. First through them, later through organized missions, Christianity came to the Vikings of Norway. Then Norway's first Christian ruler, Olaf, was himself martyred.

In the last century a delegation of Norwegian Christians visited Holy Island to say sorry for the violence inflicted by their forebears and to offer a hand of reconciliation. As a sign that, with the martyrdom of their king, their country, too, had entered into 'the fellowship of suffering', they presented a bust of Olaf's head to Holy Island's church, and this is now displayed in the north aisle. The Declaration of these peace-makers is framed and displayed in the vestry. It states that they came with contrite hearts to honour the sacrifices of those early Lindisfarne monks and to pray that our common memories will help us to walk in the paths of the Lord in the future, for 'pilgrimage is . . . the openness to be changed in spirit and to search for new values'.

Matthew 5:38–42

Lead us from fear to trust
Lead us from despair to hope
Lead us from hate to love
Lead us from war to peace.
Deep peace of the Son of peace
Fill our hearts, our workplace, our world.

The International Peace Prayer (adapted)

*

Week 2: Evening

O Christ, Son of the living God
May your holy angels guard our sleep
May they watch over us as we rest
And hover around our beds.
Let them reveal to us in our dreams
Visions of your glorious truth.
May no fears or worries delay
Our willing, prompt repose.

Psalm 84
1 Timothy 3:14–16

Child of Humanity
Trinity's only Son
Gentle and strong
From whose line we were born
Bring your peace to your warring children
Peace between enemies
Peace within families
Peace in our streets
Peace in our hearts.

In the whirling wheels of the world you are with us
When the day takes its toll you are with us
In the clamour of strife you are with us
When the world turns sour you are with us
When we go to our rest you are with us.

*

Week 3: Morning

Babe of heaven, Defenceless Love,
You had to travel far from your home;
Strengthen us on our pilgrimage of trust on earth.
King of glory, you accepted such humbling;
Clothe us with the garments of humility.
Your birth shows us the simplicity of the Father's
    love;
Keep us in the simplicity of that love.
Your coming shows us the wonder of being human;
Help us to cherish every human life.

Psalm 82
Micah 4:1–4

Tuesday: *Peace*

This is not an easy peace I would give you, my children. It cost me the cross to reconcile you to my Father. You must humble yourselves before each other, listen to each other's pain, share your brother's burden, seek his forgiveness, if you would really be reconciled in my love and my way.

Myrtle Kerr[9]

May our nation find your will as her destiny.
May our nation find God-guided representatives at
    home and abroad.
May our nation find peace within itself
and become a peace-maker in the international
    family.

Frank Buckman

Deep peace of the Spirit to you
Peace of the air flowing out to you
Peace of the Son growing strong in you.

*

Week 3: Midday reflection at the lime kilns

The best-preserved nineteenth-century lime kilns in the north-east of England stand by the shore beyond the castle. They remind us that for generations Holy Island echoed to the sound of hard industrial labour. The white-hot heat of the kilns purified the raw material. Trains transported and boats exported the lime.

Every human being is born to work. It is a noble thing. But sometimes it becomes demeaning. We must stand in solidarity with everyone in the world who works in degrading conditions.

Work should not be degrading, but it should be testing. In my garden is a potter's kiln. It reminds me, when my work is testing, to remember God's word to Jeremiah: 'I am like a potter who puts people into my kiln in order to make them better and purer.'

Jeremiah 18:1–11

Creator God
The raw materials are yours
The energy is yours
The skills are yours
Those we work with are yours.
Work is your gift.
Into your hands we place
Our materials
Our energies
Our skills
Our colleagues.
You are our reward.

*

Week 3: Evening

Lighten our darkness at the end of the day
Defend us from perils, our fears allay
Lighten our burdens, bring joy to our rest
And grant, on our waking, we give you our best.

Psalm 85
Matthew 11:15

Souls of prayer are souls of deep silence. That is why we must accustom ourselves to deep stillness of the soul.

Tuesday: *Peace*

God is the friend of silence. See how nature, the trees, the flowers, the grass grow in deep silence. See how the stars, the moon, and the sun move in silence. The more we receive in our silent prayer, the more we can give in our active life. . . . Jesus is waiting for us in the silence. It is there that he speaks to our souls.

Mother Teresa

At the drawing in of the day may your contemplations bring you peace.

May the soft mists of God's presence wrap you in their gentle folds.

May the light of God's presence lengthen you.

May the might of God's presence strengthen you.

May the warmth of God's presence restore you.

May all that God has sowed in your life flower and ripen.

May God's harvest in your life be fruitful and abundant.[10]

*

Week 4: Morning

Glory to the most High God who has come to live among us

Glory to the One who journeys with us now.

Eternal Light shine into our hearts

Eternal Goodness deliver us from evil

Eternal Power strengthen us

Eternal Wisdom scatter the darkness of our ignorance

Eternal Pity have mercy on us

Tuesday: *Peace*

With our whole being we shall seek your face
Until we are brought to your holy Presence.

After Alcuin

Psalm 122
Isaiah 11:1–5

Listen . . .
   to the fragile feelings, not to the clashing fury
   to the quiet sounds, not to the loud clamour
   to the steady heartbeat, not to the noisy confusion
   to the hidden voices, not to the obvious chatter
   to the deep harmonies, not to the surface discord.

Anonymous

Peace between factions
Peace between neighbours
Peace between lovers
In love of the King of Life.

Peace between peoples
Peace between races
Peace between generations
In love of the King of Life.

*

Week 4: Midday reflection by the harbour

The Gospel story of Jesus sleeping peacefully while his
disciples panic on their storm-tossed boat is a lesson for

us at all times. The early Christians on Holy Island show us a way of putting this lesson into practice.

A delegation from Lindisfarne once had to travel far south by boat and bring back the princess who was to marry Northumbria's king. The delegation's leader, Utta, begged Aidan to pray for their safe keeping during this hazardous and significant journey. Aidan gave them a jar of consecrated oil to take with them. He predicted that they would encounter storms, but that the winds would drop as soon as they poured the oil on the troubled waters.

On the return journey a storm did indeed blow up. It was so fierce that the boat began to sink and the frightened crew thought they would perish – until they remembered Aidan's words and the oil. They poured it over the pounding waves and the storm subsided. This story is the origin of the time-honoured phrase, 'to pour oil on troubled waters'.

The world often seems to be a sea of troubles. Let us learn, in our prayers, to pour oil on troubled waters.

Luke 8:22–25

We bring to you the troubles of the world
Calm us, and help us rest in you
We bring to you the troubles in our households
Calm us, and help us rest in you
We bring to you the troubles in our church
Calm us, and help us rest in you
We bring to you the troubles of the world
Calm us, and help us rest in you.

*

Week 4: Evening

Guardian of the planets
Kindler of the stars
We pass into the darkness
Encompassed by you.
Protect us through the hours of this night,
be they silent or stormy,
that we who are wearied by the changes and chances
    of this restless world
may rest upon your eternal changelessness.

Psalm 115
Luke 2:25–32

Elderly people like ourselves frequently make attempts
to amend their behaviour, hoping that God will forgive
them past sins and judge them on present goodness.
God will not be swayed by that kind of calculation. It is
the heart, not the mind, that needs to change: we must
learn to love God more fully. And love coming from the
heart makes no calculation. If a person loves God with
his whole heart, he will entrust himself to God's love,
without seeking to sway God's judgement by displays
of good behaviour. If my heart could change in such a
way, my fear of death would disappear.

Pelagius[11]

Sleep in peace.
Sleep soundly.
Sleep in love.
May the Weaver of dreams
Weave well in you as you sleep.

*

Week 5: Morning

Peace between victor and vanquished
Peace between old and young
Peace between rich and poor
The peace of Christ above all.

Psalm 89:5–18
Luke 6:27–36

Always keep God's peace and love among you, and when you have to seek guidance about your affairs, take great care to be of one mind. Live in mutual good-will also with Christ's other servants. . . . Never think you are superior to other people who share your faith and way of life.

Cuthbert's last words

Christ be within me
Christ be beside me
Christ in the stranger
Christ in the friend
Christ in my speaking
Christ in my thinking
Christ in my working
Christ at my end.

May you see the face of Christ in everyone you meet.
May everyone you meet see the face of Christ in you.

*

Tuesday: *Peace*

Week 5: Midday reflection
looking towards Farne Isle

An old Celtic word for prayer meant literally 'the quiet of Christ'. Silence, observed Thomas Carlyle, 'is the element in which great things fashion themselves together.' The Celtic Christians learned the value of silence from the desert fathers and mothers.

Cuthbert, who, in the busy life of Lindisfarne, would sometimes snatch hours for prayer from the still nights, finally entered into the 'desert' of the Inner Farne island, which one can see from Lindisfarne's southern shore. Bede enthuses that Cuthbert was delighted that 'after a long and spotless active life he should be thought worthy to ascend to the stillness of Divine contemplation.' But the original *Life of Cuthbert*, written by an anonymous monk at Lindisfarne, makes the point that Cuthbert succeeded in living a contemplative life in the midst of an active life.

There is a contemplative in all us, which we sometimes discover when we get away from our routine or when we retire. Michael Burden discovered a way of contemplating after he retired to Holy Island. Each morning he gathers driftwood from the shores, which he thinks of as 'a gift from the sea, carried by nature, to reveal hidden truths', and he crafts it into 'driftwood icons'. He has written the following prayer, to be said when contemplating a driftwood icon:

Lord Jesus Christ, our God and King, enlighten and direct the mind of your servant as s/he comes to contemplate the driftwood you have allowed to be washed up upon the shore of Holy Island. As you took body in the womb of the Blessed Virgin for the salvation of humankind, so may I take spiritual body in the womb created by this contemplation, so that I can experience eternity and rest in your tranquillity.

[s]Michael Burden

Lamentations 3:22–29

Lord, a thousand voices call to me this day.
Help me to filter out sound-bites and slogans, images
    and screens,
conversations and traffic, newspapers and internet . . .
and to turn away all that is not of you,
and to recognize and hold on to
all that is of you.

Babe of Heaven
strengthen us on our pilgrimage.
Your birth shows us
the simplicity of the Father's love
the wonder of being human.
Help us to live fully human lives for you.
We quieten our souls under the stillness of sky
and we nestle with you in the Father's lap.

*

Week 5: Evening

The peace of the Spirit be mine this night,
The peace of the Son be mine this night,
The peace of the Father be mine this night,

Tuesday: *Peace*

The peace of all peace be mine this night,
Each morning and evening of my life.

Psalm 2
Isaiah 9:6–7

This night is the long night
It will snow and it will drift
White snow there will be till day
White moon there will be till morn
This night is the eve of the Great Nativity
This night is born Mary Virgin's Son
This night is born Jesus, Son of the King of Glory
This night is born to us the root of our joy
This night gleamed the sun of the mountains high
This night gleamed sea and shore together
This night was born Christ the King of greatness.
Ere 'twas heard that the Glory was come
Heard was the wave upon the strand.
Ere 'twas heard that his foot had reached earth
Heard was the song of the angels glorious.
This night is the long night.

Carmina Gadelica

Glowed to Him wood and tree
Glowed to Him mount and sea
Glowed to Him land and plain
When that His foot was come to earth.

Carmina Gadelica

Peace be upon our breath
Peace be upon our eyes
Peace be upon our sleep.

Wednesday

Mission

A Holy Island map

Wednesday: *Mission*

Display panels in St Mary's Church explain how Christianity spread from early Irish churches to Lindisfarne. The Priory Museum tells compellingly how it spread from Lindisfarne to the English-speaking people in the north, the middle and even the south of Britain.

The story of how English-speaking people were first transformed from bloodthirsty barbarians into caring Christians is well worth telling. Two ways of mission were tried among the English. At two Northumberland sites, Yeavering and Ladywell, near Rothbury, Paulinus, the Roman chaplain to Northumbria's Queen, held mass instruction and baptisms before Aidan's Mission began. It seems he only engaged in mission when he accompanied the king to the royal centres. Mission was an extension of monarchy, a kind of religious civil service. This may be described as 'top-down, one-shape-fits-all' mission. When the king was killed, most of the people whom Paulinus had evangelized went back to paganism. That kind of mission only went skin deep.

Aidan, on the other hand, although he could do nothing without the consent of the new King Oswald, had a grass-roots approach. He sought out people where they were, far away from the royal presence, and made himself vulnerable in so doing. He took time with individuals, drew out their own concerns, and shared himself and his worldly goods with them as well as his message.

Wednesday: *Mission*

The Mission begun by Aidan was not just a message. The message was modelled at the monastery, which sent out faith-sharing teams who lived the message wherever they went. Thus Cuthbert healed the sick and even prayed for sick babies in plague-ridden villages. This kind of mission did not depend on human power, but it did depend on the power of God's Holy Spirit. Through constant prayer and Scripture meditation the missionaries invited God to work in the lives of the people.

The Holy Spirit, mission and healing are inseparable.

Wednesday: *Mission*

Week 1: Morning

Great Creator of the blood-red moon and falling
  stars
Great Saviour of the miraculous birth and rising
  from death
Great Spirit of the seers and sacred words
Come into our minds
Come into our mouths
Come into our deeds
Until we become your presence and sign.

Psalm 139:1–12
Isaiah 61:1–3

E. Stanley Jones, the missionary to India, once asked
Mahatma Gandhi: 'How can we make the Christian
faith more native to India, so that it is no longer something "foreign" which is associated with foreign governments and seen as foreign religious practice, but it
becomes part of life in India and a faith that makes a
powerful contribution to building up this country?'

Gandhi replied: 'Firstly, I would suggest that all
Christians – missionaries and others – must start living
more like Christ. Secondly, practise your faith without
blurring it or watering it down. Thirdly, put special
emphasis on love because it is the central point of
Christian faith and therefore the decisive motivating
force. Fourthly, study non-Christian religions with
great sympathy, so that you can appeal to people of
other faiths more effectively.'

Set us free, O God, to cross barriers for you,
as you crossed barriers for us.

Wednesday: *Mission*

Spirit of God, make us open to others in listening,
generous to others in giving,
and sensitive to others in praying
through Jesus Christ our Lord.

Brother Bernard SSF

*

Week 1: Midday reflection at Cuddies Beach

The wild goose is a Celtic symbol of God's Spirit. Hundreds of migrating wild geese alight on Holy Island each year. They include Canadian Brent and Pink-footed geese. A BBC TV programme entitled *Hidden Forces* stated: 'We've only just begun to unravel some of the magnetic senses which guide the geese across the world.' Some geese return to a place after over thirty years of absence.

On Easter Day 1996 I lingered, with some sadness, outside my house with two friends. The church community which had been my family for many years had just said farewell to me. Now I faced a day of packing before moving to the unknown quantity of Lindisfarne. There was a great cry overhead. It was a wild goose. I had neither seen nor heard a wild goose in all my years in that place. The Holy Spirit was saying, 'I am going ahead of you to Lindisfarne.'

A member of the music band 'Iona' once came to Cuddies Beach. There she wrote some lyrics which became an exquisite song on their CD *Iona*: 'Here I stand . . . years have passed . . . waiting for the Wild Goose to come to me.'

Wednesday: *Mission*

John 3:1–8

Great Spirit, Wild Goose of the Almighty
Be my eye in the dark places
Be my flight in the trapped places
Be my host in the wild places
Be my formation in the lost places
Be my brood in the barren places.

*

Week 1: Evening

O Christ, you had compassion on the crowds
You drew people to yourself
You repelled none who knew they were needy.
Grant us hearts like yours
Hearts that go out in genuine greeting
    and humble welcome
Until, in the fellowship of sharing
Souls are drawn to you.

Psalm 138
Matthew 28:16–20

Patrick found a way of swimming down to the depths
of the Irish psyche and warming and transforming Irish
imagination – making it more humane and noble while
keeping it Irish.

Thomas Cahill[12]

From the rising of the sun to its going down
The Lord's name will be praised.

Wednesday: *Mission*

As the sun sets on us, let us remember
    a people on whom the sun is rising
That they may know the light of Christ.

Spirit of Truth, look down upon a world
    in thrall to lies and illusions,
Work in the darkness to bring all things into light.

*

Week 2: Morning

On those whose day is drab
Come Holy Spirit
On those who harbour fear
Come, Holy Spirit
On a parched land
Come, Holy Spirit.

Psalm 74:10–23
John 16:5–16

So it came about that Ireland, a land filled with people
who never had the knowledge of God, but worshipped
idols and other foul objects, now has a people of the
Lord who are called the children of God. It was not my
grace, but God, victorious in me, who resisted all oppo-
sition when I came to the people of Ireland to preach
the Gospel and to suffer insults from unbelievers. If I
should be worthy, I am ready to give even my life most
willingly and unhesitatingly for his Name. I am bound
by the Spirit who witnesses to me. Christ the Lord told
me to come here and stay with the people for the rest of

my life, if he so wills, and he will guard me from every evil that I might not sin before him.

St Patrick[13]

Eternal God and Father
You create us by your power
And redeem us by your love:
Guide and strengthen us by your Spirit,
That we may give ourselves in love and service
to one another and to you.

From an Anglican liturgy

*

Week 2: Midday reflection at Jenny Bell's well

At the foot of the field that slopes down towards Cuddies Beach you will see the recently restored Jenny Bell's well. Wells and springs abound in the Bible and throughout the ages as images of spiritual renewal. Genesis chapter 26 tells how Isaac restored disused wells in the lush valleys, but his people quarrelled over water rights. So Isaac, placing his faith in God, left them to it, and went up to a higher place. He need not have worried, for his folk soon dug up an upper spring. Some of those who had opposed him, observing that he moved with God, were reconciled and worked with him.

Holy Island is sometimes referred to as a place of Upper Springs – that is, a place for outreach, mission and teamwork. Wherever we live, we can be Upper Springs people if we learn to drink deeply of God himself.

Genesis 26:1–33

What would the world be
Once bereft of wet and of wildness?
Let them be left, O let them be left
Wetness and wildness.

Gerard Manley Hopkins

Calm us by your quiet pools
   Refresh us in your sparkling streams
Drench us in your powerful downfalls
   Soak us in your mighty seas.

*

Week 2: Evening

Come Holy Spirit, our souls inspire
And lighten with eternal fire.
Implant in us your grace from above,
Enter our minds and hearts with love.

O come anointing Spirit of peace
Well-spring of life and gentleness.
Past ages called you the Paraclete
To us you bring your sevenfold gifts.

You are the Power of God's right hand
Promise of God to the waiting church

Wednesday: *Mission*

Words of true life on human lips.
Illumine now our hearts anew.

Come pour your love into our souls
Refresh our weak frame with incoming strength
Give grace and courage to endure
Cast away our deadly foe.

Grant us your peace for evermore.
With you as Guide upon the way
Evil shall no more harm our souls.
We shall know as we are known.

Teach us the Trinity to know
Father, Son and Spirit, One:
The Three in One and One in Three
Now and ever, eternally.

Adapted from Veni Creator[14]

Psalm 17
Acts 2:1–12

After coming to Ireland I was put to work tending cattle, sheep and hogs, and many times during that day I
would pray. More and more the love of God and the
fear of God came to me, so that my faith was strength-
ened and my spirit was moved. In a single day I would
pray as often as a hundred times, and nearly as often at
night, when I was staying in the woods and in the
mountains. I would rouse myself before daylight to
pray, whether in snow, frost, or rain; it made no differ-
ence, and I felt no bad effects. Because the Spirit in me
was fervent, I knew no sluggishness.

St Patrick[15]

Wednesday: *Mission*

Great Spirit, who broods over the sleeping world
As we and all your children sleep this night
Restore the garment of our self-respect
And remake us in your beauty.

Renew in us as we sleep
The stillness of our being
The soundness of our bodies
And bring to dawn our wholeness.

*

Week 3: Morning

Wind of Heaven
Blow away dross and deceits
Refresh our battered souls
Brace us for what is to come.

Psalm 9:1–12
1 Peter 2:1–12

In the place of fear
God's strength to uphold me,
In the place of emptiness
God's wisdom to guide me,
In the place of confusion
God's eye for my seeing,
In the place of discord
God's ear for my hearing,
In the place of froth
God's word for my speaking,
To save me from false agendas
that harm my body or soul.

Wednesday: *Mission*

Holy Spirit release us, that we may be strong and free
Sending Spirit, empower us to reach out to others
May your church grow in holiness and in numbers.

*

Week 3: Midday reflection
on cliff ledges

There are some ledges on the edge of the Heugh which used to be called 'gunners' holes', since ammunition was kept there. More recently they have been adopted as 'prayer holes', and so they remind us of a different kind of ammunition.

When we are at the edge we see horizons which are denied to those who stay in their comfort zones.

Walking along a cliff-top our bodies and souls face
    each other
    and that is how we grow.
The edge is in fact always the centre of spiritual
    renewal.
We are called to mould the kingdoms of the earth
so that they reflect the Kingdom of Heaven.
Any Christian movement that becomes respectable
    risks being brought from the edge to the centre –
    and so risks being given the kiss of death.
How will I keep myself on the spiritual edge?

Martin Wallace

God likes to take us to the edges. Often it is only when we are willing to go to the edges that we truly meet others, for many people who are on edges of loneliness, anger, despair or adventure recognize and reach out to others who are also on an edge. Jesus allowed himself to be pushed to the edges of society. That is why he could communicate to so many ordinary people. This is how the truly precious things of life are passed on – at the edges.

Hebrews 11

When my life seems all duty and dust
In the midst of the day when we droop
When routine things turn into rust
And people from valour do stoop
Then the Wild Goose comes to my aid
His wings pass o'er and give shade
Make the day's scorching heat soon fade
And I know in God's image I'm made
And that nothing of this world can degrade
Nothing of this world can degrade.

Andrew Dick

*

Week 3: Evening

The church exists by mission, as fire exists by burning.

Emil Brunner

Kindling Spirit come,
Inflame our waiting hearts.
Anointing Spirit come,

Wednesday: *Mission*

Distribute among us your gifts –
Wisdom, understanding and strength
Knowledge, reverence and insight.

Psalm 119:137–154
Romans 10:11–15

I, too, though I am frail, desire to rise up from the sleep
of idleness, to kindle the flame of divine love, the long-
ing that is at the heart of divine compassion, and to rise
above the stars, so that God's love ever burns within
me. O that my life might be like a living flame that
burns throughout the dark night in the house of God,
giving light to all who come in from the cold.

Lord, give me that love which does not fail people;
make my life like an open fire that you are always kindling, which nothing can quench. O Saviour most
sweet, may I receive perpetual light from you, so that
the world's darkness may be driven from us. O eternal
Priest, may I see you, observe you, desire you, and love
you alone as you shine in your eternal temple.

Columbanus

Come like fire and kindle love in our hearts
Come like wind and breathe life into our frames
Come like water and flow through our souls
Come like the earth: sustain and nourish our being.

*

Week 4: Morning

For my shield this day I call
Heaven's might, Sun's brightness

Wednesday: *Mission*

Moon's whiteness
Fire's glory
Lightning's swiftness
Wind's wildness
Ocean's depth
Earth's solidity
Rock's immobility.

From St Patrick's Breastplate

Psalm 62
Ephesians 4:1–13

Jesus has gathered us, is gathering us, and will gather us
out of all regions, till he should make resurrection of
our hearts from the earth, and teach us that we are all
of one substance, and members of one another.

Columbanus[16]

Perfect Comforter! Wonderful Refreshment!
You make peace to dwell in our soul.
   In our labour, you offer rest;
   In temptation, strength.
From heaven shine forth with your glorious light.

Taizé

Into the life of the Three I immerse you
May their breath be yours to live
May their love be yours to give.

*

Week 4: Midday reflection at the eating places

Lindisfarne has four hotels with bars and restaurants plus a cafe or two. On occasions like the Jazz Festival or New Year's Night it is customary to visit each place. In the low season island residents attend quizzes or other events at these places. Until licensing laws were relaxed a few years ago, the island was a haven for people who looked for pubs that did not close at the normal times.

Eating and drinking are important social occasions. They provide contexts where we can open up to one another simply for the joy of meeting. When Jesus made water taste like good wine (John 2), the need being met was a neighbourhood celebration whose 'swing' was threatened – an extended family's good name for hospitality was in the balance.

Food and drink provided without the hospitality of the heart is half-baked. It is surely no accident that Jesus so often taught or did works of mercy in the setting of a meal. But he not only shared bread; he shared himself. The kingdom of God has been likened to a party. Let's go for it!

Isaiah 25:1–8

Bless, O God, the food we eat
and if there be any poor creature
hungry or thirsty walking along the road

send them in to us that we can share the food with
    them
just as you share your gifts with all of us.

A traditional Irish grace

*

Week 4: Evening

We saw a stranger yesterday
We put food in the eating place
Drink in the drinking place
Music in the listening place
And with the sacred name of the triune God
He blessed us and our house
Our cattle and our dear ones.
As the lark says in her song:
Often, often, often goes the Christ
In the stranger's guise.

A Celtic rune of hospitality

Psalm 23
Mark 8:14–21

I would prepare a feast and be host to the great High
    King,
with all the company of heaven.
The sustenance of pure love be in my house,
the roots of repentance in my house.
Baskets of love be mine to give,
with cups of mercy for all the company.
Sweet Jesus, be there with us, with all the company of
    heaven.

Wednesday: *Mission*

May cheerfulness abound in the feast,
the feast of the great High King,
my host for all eternity.

Traditional[17]

May the blessing of light be on you
light without light and light within.
May it warm your heart
till it glows like a great peat fire
so that the stranger may come and warm herself at it
as well as the friend.
And may the light shine out of your eyes
like a candle set in the windows of a house.

Traditional Irish (adapted)

*

Week 5: Morning

From false desires and selfish deeds
All-knowing God, deliver us
From unworthy thoughts and prideful claims
All-seeing God, deliver us
From unclean hearts and petty ways
All-cleansing God, deliver us.

Psalm 27
James 5:13–16

A cause of grief is sin
A cause of anguish is death
A cause of joy is repentance
And cleansing in the river of health.

Carmina Gadelica

Wednesday: *Mission*

Always
A mind has sought you
An eye has seen you
A mouth has named you
A heart has desired you.

We receive the power of the Creator of life
We receive the power of the Christ of love
We receive the help of the Holy Spirit
Who together bring us to wholeness.

*

Week 5: Midday reflection at Emmanuel Head

Emmanuel Head is the white triangle at the tip of the uninhabited end of the island. To the left of it lie Castlehead Rocks. In the bad old days hard-pressed fishermen made a living by lighting fires on this promontory. Ships sailing close by at night thought these were beacons to guide them in, and were shipwrecked. The canny locals lived off the plunder. In order to end this bad practice Emmanuel Head was erected and painted in white to show clearly that this was a zone that boats should avoid.

Smuggling has been a part of Holy Island's story. Smuggling thrives when people feel that there is no one out there you can trust to do their best for you. Is it more than coincidence that the white beacon was named Emmanuel Head? For 'Emmanuel' means 'God with us'. God is indeed with us, and for us, whether our need is for food or for safety. God always guides us in ways that are for our good and inspires us to be good neighbours.

Isaiah 30:19–26

Guide me, O thou great Redeemer,
Pilgrim through this barren land.
I am weak, but thou art mighty;
Hold me with thy powerful hand.
Bread of heaven, feed me now and evermore.

W. Williams

*

Week 5: Evening

In the name of the God of wholeness
In the name of Compassion's Son
In the name of the healing Spirit
Tonight may we be one.

For the ways we have marred your image in us,
forgive us.
For resentment, rush or lack of trust, forgive us.
Now we open ourselves in love and faith to your
healing presence.

Psalm 51
Galatians 5:16–26

Cuthbert became famous for his miracles. Through his persistent prayers he restored to health many who were sick, he cured some that were afflicted by unclean spirits, not only when present . . . praying, touching, commanding and exorcising, but also when absent either by prayer alone or even indeed by predicting their cure . . . . Signs and wonders whereby he shone outwardly gave witness to the inward virtues of his mind.

Bede[18]

May the Divine Father make us instruments of
    healing
May the Complete Christ remove what hinders
    healing
May the Holy Spirit give us power for healing.

Healing Christ, you walk the world with those who
    suffer
in broken places of the world.

We come to you with our wounds and theirs.

Encircle those for whom we pray
Enter their body, mind and spirit
And heal them of all that harms.

Peace and blessing from the Spirit
And from the Three who are ever One.

Thursday

Community

A fisherman at the harbour

Thursday: *Community*

It was on a Thursday that Jesus prayed for unity, spoke about himself, his divine Father and the Spirit as a Co-Unity in God (John 14—17) and instituted Holy Communion. Community is at the heart of God, and Holy Communion is community at the heart of the world. That is why we pray for community and unity on Thursdays.

Since the destruction of New York's Twin Towers on 11 September 2001 some young, religionless Westerners have become Muslims. What draws them to this faith? Perhaps it is the Islamic idea of 'God's will in all of life'. They think Christians are individualistic and have given up on the idea that human beings should live as a community of justice. Or they think Christianity has made the doctrine of God too complicated; that churches with signs saying they worship Jesus as Lord cannot be worshipping the one God of all people.

A visiting Christian priest told me he spent his days on Holy Island meditating on this fact: that at the very time when Mohammed met Arab Christians who did not understand the Trinity, and whom he thought worshipped three gods, Celtic Christians were intensely aware of the Triune God. What would have happened, he wondered, if Mohammed had met Aidan and Cuthbert?

A Sufi Muslim told me that only Christ can unite Christians, Jews and Muslims. Why? Because he had a

Thursday: *Community*

Jewish mother, and Jews follow their mothers; Christians are his adherents and are supposed to do what he says; and when he comes again he will teach them all to pray the Muslim way – that is, to fast and pray in rhythm with the sun's rising and setting.

The Koran teaches that God is all-compassionate. Christians believe God's compassion is so complete that it can even be incarnate in human life. That is why Cuthbert shed tears from his heart when, in Holy Communion, he re-lived the self-giving of God in the form of Christ on the Cross. Post-Twin Towers seekers after God need to see that quality of God reflected in the Christians they meet.

Celtic-style Christians do fast and pray in the rhythms of the sun. They do not detach Christ from the Trinity, as have some Western Protestants. They see God's Presence in all of life and are single-minded about letting God's will hold sway. They believe in community.

Bear these thoughts in mind as you make these Thursday prayers your own.

Week 1: Morning

Thrice holy God, eternal Three in One
Make your people holy, make your people one
Stir up in us the flame that burns out pride and power
Restore in us the trust that brings the servant heart to
  flower.
Thrice holy God, come as the morning dew
Inflame in us your love
That draws all lesser loves to you.

Psalm 133
John 14: 9–17

Deep within all of us dwells the Blessed Trinity. At the
depth of our being the Father continually loves the Son,
while the Son responds to the Father in love and prayer
through the Holy Spirit. In our prayer of meditation we
desire to be part of the love and prayer of Jesus to the
Father. Rather than think up words or aspirations or
images of our own, we wish to unite ourselves with the
loving prayer going on continually within us. In this
prayer we also seek to open ourselves completely to the
Holy Spirit, that the Holy Spirit may bring about in us
conversion, repentance and faith in the Good News of
Jesus Christ.

From Ireland[19]

May we bear the marks of the friendship of God
God above us
God beside us
God beneath us
Trinity of Love.

Thursday: *Community*

Father cherish me
Son cherish me
Spirit cherish me
Three all-kindly.

Creator make me holy
Saviour make me holy
Spirit make me holy
Three all-holy.

Make me aware, dear God, of
the eye that beholds me
the hand that holds me
the heart that loves me
the Presence that enfolds me.

*

Week 1: Midday reflection
by a walled cornfield

In summer a number of Holy Island's fields are full of
swaying corn. They bring to mind words from ancient
Christian liturgy which are often repeated at the
Thursday Eucharist at St Mary's: 'As the grain once
scattered in the fields and the grapes once dispersed on
the hillside are now reunited on this table in bread and
wine, so, Lord, may your whole people soon be gathered together from the four corners of the earth into
your kingdom.'

Cornfields and sheep-fields are often protected by
walls built of stone without cement. One day a visitor
from a healing centre took a photograph of a piece of
wall which had long been broken down, but recently

some stones had been replaced and the wall was being built up again. He meditated upon this. The wholeness and unity which marked the early Saxon community had been broken down, he suggested, but now God was restoring what had been divided. Person by person, stone by stone, the community was being rebuilt in unity.

People who want their own way, or who are empire builders, or who dismiss other people, are like the crumbling wall. People who want to build one another up, and to do right by God in a natural way, are like the restored wall. 'The restored wall is coming', the visitor said.

Whether we know it or not, we come from one Source, and we belong to one another. But we have become fragmented. Only a miracle can move us from fragmentation to unity. That miracle is possible. It is in our midst.

1 Corinthians 12:12–26

Ground of all being, all peoples come from you.
May we honour one another and seek the common
   good.
Reconciler of all people, employers, employees
   and shareholders are like fingers on your hand.
May the wealth and work of the world be available
   to all
   and for the exploitation of none.
Unity of the world, from you all peace, all justice
   flow.
May we respect the rule of law and cherish the web
   of life.

*

Week 1: Evening

Creator who birthed the world,
    breathe your life into us.
Saviour who entered the world,
    stretch out your hand to us.
Spirit who pervades the world,
    fill and overflow us.

Psalm 48
John 17:20–23

'I see! I see!
What do I see?
Three in One, and One in Three
And all the Three are all for me!
All for *me*!'

                A dying and previously dumb
                      Scottish Christian[20]

Day has ended
Father, guard us sleeping
Night has come
Saviour, guard us sleeping
Our minds need calm
Spirit, guard us sleeping
Look on us, O God
Father, guard us sleeping
Warm us, O God
Saviour, guard us sleeping
We rest in you, O God
Spirit, guard us sleeping.

*

Week 2: Morning

For my shield this day I call:
A mighty power, the Holy Trinity
Faith in the Three, trust in the One
Creating all through love.

In faith I trust in the Father of all:
He's my refuge, a very strong wall.

For my shield this day I call:
Christ's power in his coming
Christ's power in his dying
Christ's power in his rising.

For my shield this day I call:
The mighty Spirit who breathes through all
Faith in the Three, trust in the One
Creating all through love.

Psalm 12
Philippians 2:1–11

Always keep God's peace and love among you, and
when you have to seek guidance about your affairs,
take great care to be of one mind. Live in mutual good-
will also with Christ's other servants, and do not
despise Christians who come to you for hospitality, but
see that you welcome them, give them accommodation,
and send them on their way with friendship and kindness.

Cuthbert's last words

Thursday: *Community*

Circle the world, Lord
Keep fear without, keep friendship within.
Circle the world, Lord
Keep wrong without, keep right within.
Circle the world, Lord
Keep greed without, keep generosity within.

May the blessing of the Three who are One be in
Your working and speaking
Your meeting and making
Your laughing and crying
Your eating and resting.

*

Week 2: Midday reflection at the Heritage Centre

Several people were involved in producing the book that we call the Lindisfarne Gospels, including Bishop Eadfrith, Ethilwald, Billfrith the Anchorite and Aldred. This treasure is now accessible to everyone in digital form at Lindisfarne's Heritage Centre.

The pigments for the colouring of the Gospels came from diverse lands. The vellum on which they were written came from the skins of many young calves. The scribe had an eye for the minutest details and knew how to draw out for the reader the meaning of the sacred text. Underneath the Latin was a translation in early English, one of the first examples of the English language.

After many years Lindisfarne once again has a Scriptorium, called The Burning Light, where beautiful illumination is being created by Mary Fleeson. You will find it on the same road as the Heritage Centre.

Luke 13:18–21

Creator of night and day
Lead us from dark to light
Lead us from ugliness to beauty
Lead us from stagnation to creativity
Lead us from ourselves to you.

*

Week 2: Evening

We give you thanks, Kindly Light, that you led our forebears in the Faith through a cloud by day and a fire by night, and that you always lead your people on. We give you thanks that you have led us to this place. Pour forth your kindness on your people, Father, Saviour, and radiant Spirit.

Psalm 105:1–11
Acts 1:1–5

Triune God who mothers us all
Nurture the people through your church:
Through her pastors
Nourish us
Through her teachers
Establish us
Through her prophets
Envision us
Through her musicians

Thursday: *Community*

Inspire us
Through her saints
Sanctify us
Through her givers
Bless us.

Lord, you have called us to serve you
In the midst of the world's affairs.
When we stumble, hold us
When we fall, raise us
When we are pressed with evil, deliver us
When we turn aside from good, restore us
And bring us at last to your glory.

Alcuin[21]

*

Week 3: Morning

Birther of the human race
You summon the day to dawn
And call us to live in communion.

Lord Jesus Christ, Light of the world,
By your cross you have overcome all darkness that
   oppresses.
Come and shine on us in our communities
That we may grow and live together in your love
Which makes us one with all humanity.

Psalm 80
Matthew 18:15–20

Thursday: *Community*

There is a sense in which Europe is the creation of the monks who journeyed into the darkness with this Celtic way of seeing, for the light that troubled their dreams had to shine *into* the darkness; it was a Christian light, incarnate, sacrificial. It was a light and a vision that had been tested and purified and deepened in the darkness of Gethsemane and Calvary, a light breaking forth from the Cross, an Easter light, a vision of the Risen Lord who was 'the Son of the gentle Mary'.

Noel O'Donohue[22]

> Great Christ, you prayed for the unity of all who believe;
> May your churches, rejoicing in the communion of heaven,
>> attain communion round one table.
>
> Great Christ, you call us to love our neighbours;
> May our local communities seek the common good.
> Great Christ, through bread and wine you give us signs
>> of your Presence transforming all creation;
>
> May the media and creative artists glimpse this vision,
>> and reflect it to the world.

*

Week 3: Midday reflection at the castle

Lindisfarne's castle, which was restored by Lutchens, is a masterpiece which seems to grow out of the impregnable rock on which it is built. It looks across the sea to that even more impregnable castle, Bamburgh.

At that site King Oswald once invited Aidan to celebrate an Easter banquet with him. A silver dish was placed on the table full of rich foods. Aidan had just raised his hand to ask a blessing on the food when the king's officer for the welfare of the poor informed him that a crowd of needy people from every district was outside asking alms of the king. Oswald at once ordered the dainties which had been set in front of him to be carried to the poor, the large silver dish to be broken up, and the pieces to be divided amongst them. Aidan was deeply moved by this.

It is thought that this incident is the origin of the custom whereby the British monarch gives silver coins to deserving people on Maundy Thursday.

Oswald was probably the first English ruler to appoint staff for the welfare of the poor. He had introduced Christ's ways of compassion and justice into the greedy, ruthless politics of his time. In the heat of our day let us seek the God of justice.

Micah 6:6–8

Deliver the oppressed, pity the unnoticed
Raise the fallen, show yourself to the needy
Heal the sick, bring back those who have strayed
Feed the hungry, lift up the weak
Remove the prisoners' chains.
May every people come to know that you are God
That Jesus Christ is your Child
That we are your people.

Clement of Rome[23]

*

Week 3: Evening

We offer to you, Lord, the troubles of this day;
we lay down our burdens at your feet.
Forgive us our sins, give us your peace,
and help us to receive your Word.

Psalm 125
John 17:1–19

All humankind are one vast family
this world our home.
We sleep beneath one roof,
the starry sky.
We warm ourselves before one hearth,
the blazing sun.
Upon one floor of soil we stand
and breathe one air
and drink one water
and walk the night
beneath one luminescent moon.
The children of one God we are
brothers and sisters of one blood
and members in one worldwide family of God.[24]

On your world, Lord
Your love descend this night
On your church, Lord
Your love descend this night
On all who work, Lord
Your love descend this night
Where there is strife, Lord
Your love descend this night

Thursday: *Community*

Where there is neglect, Lord
Your love descend this night
On all who sleep, Lord
Your love descend this night.

*

Week 4: Morning

High King of the universe
Restore in us the image of your love
    that the longings of our hearts may be true.

Great Spirit, bring to harvest the fragments of our
    lives
Penetrate the storehouse of our memories,
    making them whole and holy.

Psalm 68:1–10
John 6:1–15

Be gentle when you touch bread.
Let it not lie, uncared for, unwanted.
So often bread is taken for granted.
There is such beauty in bread –
Beauty of sun and soil,
Beauty of patient toil.
Wind and rain have caressed it,
Christ often blessed it.
Be gentle when you touch it.

Anonymous

Source of all
We turn to you

Saviour of all
We turn to you
Sustainer of all
We turn to you.

God direct our hours
Protect our assets
Still our hearts.

*

Week 4: Midday reflection at the Village Hall

The Village Hall is an institution and is dear to people of all ages and backgrounds on the island. At the time of writing there are plans to replace the old hall with a new one suitable for the twenty-first century.

I especially enjoy the custom of inviting every household on the island to celebrate someone's special anniversary. Often there is singing, dancing, eating, drinking, conversation and comedy. It reminds me that, according to Jesus, the kingdom of God is like a party.

Matthew 22:1–14

May this place echo with the sounds of gladness
May the feasting and the friendship overflow
May the old enjoy the young and the young enjoy the
  old
And may all the people say 'Amen'.

Thursday: *Community*

May the dogs' tails wag and the birds chirp for joy
May the angels laugh at what they see
May our hearts be grateful and may God be our host
And may all the people say 'Amen'.

*

Week 4: Evening

We thank you for your presence through the day
And for friends who have helped us on our way.
As shadows fall
And the wheels of the world grow still
Forgive us for our failures in love.

Psalm 111
Romans 12:9–21

Support us, Lord
All the day long of this troubled life
Until the shadows lengthen
And evening comes
The busy world is hushed
The fever of life is over
And our work is done.
Then, Lord, in your mercy
Grant us a safe lodging
A holy rest
And peace at the last.

Traditional

God with us lying down
God with us rising up
Christ with us sleeping

Thursday: *Community*

Christ with us waking
Spirit with us now
Spirit with us evermore.

*

Week 5: Morning

Lord Jesus Christ, Light of the world,
By your cross you have overcome all darkness that
    oppresses.
Come and shine on us here
That we may grow and live together in your love
Which makes us one with all humanity.

Psalm 76
Matthew 25:31–46

May petty ways drop from us like scales until
We seek the greatness of others
We rejoice in being givers
Heaven delights in our pleasure.

Help us
To guard our words
To overcome hostility with love
To make peace
In love of the King of Life.

May I be bold in the love of God,
Strong in the peace of God,
Rich in the mercy of God.

Brian Frost

*

Week 5: Midday reflection at the Snook

Fishing lies at the heart of Lindisfarne. Over the centuries its fishermen have braved all weathers and eked a living from the sea. It is sometimes fulfilling but is always hard work. And, with the vagaries of modern fishing quotas as well as the weather, it is a precarious living.

Halfway along the causeway is the Snook and opposite, a tower. Both of these are now homes, but once they were used for the salmon industry. The salmon were gutted and boxed in the big house. The nets were dried in the tower.

The leader of Jesus' twelve apostles has been nicknamed 'The Big Fisherman'. He knew what it was to work hard for little return. But by giving himself to One greater than himself, he became fruitful in human and eternal ways that he had never before dreamed of.

John 21:1–14

O helper of those who toil and ruler of those who do
   good
Protect those who are faithful
Raise up the lowly and cast down the mighty.
Pure life-source of all who live
Light-giver and Father of lights
You shine with eternal light
You do not deny us the strength we need.
As we row trembling through the storms of this age
Christ, draw us after you to the beautiful haven of
   endless life.

Thursday: *Community*

From the envy of foes lead us to the joy of paradise
That we may hymn you for ever, O Christ,
who lives and reigns for ever.

After Columba

*

Week 5: Evening

Guardian of the night
Pour into the empty cups of the world
the beauty and blessings of Christ.
May you who laboured in love to create all life
continue creating within us new vision, new life.

Psalm 114
Romans 5:1–5

To live content with small means
To seek elegance rather than luxury
And refinement rather than fashion
To be worthy, not respectable
And wealthy, not rich
To study hard, think quietly, talk gently, act frankly
To listen to stars and birds, babes and sages, with
    open heart
To bear all cheerfully
Do all bravely
Await occasions, hurry never
In a word, to let the spiritual, unbidden and
    unconscious
Grow up through the common.
This is to be my symphony.

William Ellery Channing

Thursday: *Community*

Lord, we of this day are children of confusion;
restore the vision of God to us.
The noise of the city deafens us to the still small
    voice;
restore the hearing of God to us.
The pace of modern living chokes us;
restore the alertness of God to us.
The pride of modern living imprisons us;
restore the liberty of God to us.

The Community of Aidan and Hilda

Kindle in our hearts, O God
The flame of that love which never ceases,
That it may burn in us this night
Till we shine for ever in your presence.

Friday

The Cross

The Market Cross and landmine

Friday: *The Cross*

Jesus Christ, Son of God, died on a Friday while nailed to a Cross. On Fridays we make ourselves one with Christ's sufferings and with the suffering people of the world.

The first Christians on Holy Island learned from Aidan to eat no meals on Fridays until dusk, the time when Christ was declared dead and taken down from the Cross. This was their way of being in solidarity with Christ and of finding time to meditate on it. Some Christians observe this practice still.

There was a cross in the heart of God before there was a cross on the hill outside Jerusalem. The broad beams on which the universe is built are in the shape of a cross. The Cross, the ultimate expression of the law of self-sacrifice, runs like a scarlet thread through the Bible, through human experience, and through all creation.

The tragedy of the second millennium was that the Cross, starting with the Crusades, became an emblem of the sword, and millions of Muslims, Jews and others still think of it as such. The challenge of this third millennium is to let it be what it was and what it still is in its origin – an emblem of unconditional love.

Cuthbert, we are told, shed tears from the heart when he re-enacted in the Eucharist the life of Christ outpoured on the Cross. The gentle, unconditional love of the first Lindisfarne missionaries is the true way of the Cross. It was reflected in their ceaseless prayer of the heart, and we seek to reflect it in the prayers that follow.

Friday: *The Cross*

Week 1: Morning

Jesus, you were driven to the sands by the searching
    Spirit
Strip from us what is not of you
Forgive us for our selfish deeds, our empty speech
    and the words with which we wound
Forgive us for our false desires, our vengeful attitudes
    and for what we have left untended.

Psalm 22
Isaiah 53

Jesus' seven last sentences on the Cross

Father, forgive them; for they know not what they
    do.
Truly, I say to you, today you will be with me in
    paradise.
He is your son; she is your mother.
My God, my God, why have you forsaken me?
I am thirsty.
It is finished.
Father, into your hands I commit my spirit.

In union with witnesses and martyrs of Christ
In communion with all who have died in the faith of
    Christ
We commit ourselves to our living God
As we struggle to be faithful to you and establish
    justice.
We bring to you those who are in chains
We bring to you people who are persecuted or
    oppressed,
the homeless, the hungry and those in grinding
    poverty

Friday: *The Cross*

We bring to you those who are in pain behind closed
  doors.
Lord Jesus, you were released from the pain of the
  Cross
In you may those who suffer find release.
We bring to you those who are locked into hatred
Calm their hatred and fill their hearts and ours with
  generous love.

*

Week 1: Midday reflection at the Boiler House Chapel

To the rear of Holy Island's St Cuthbert's Centre is a
tiny chapel which was once the boilerhouse of the
Presbyterian church. On the wall there is something
unusual to look at. The person who made it went to the
former rubbish dump, which is now the beach opposite
Cuthbert's Isle. Fragments of brick and crockery which
had been dumped there were cleaned and smoothed by
the sea. Our artist collected these fragments and created a mosaic from them in the shape of a cross, and it is
this which now adorns the chapel's wall.

This is a parable for us as individuals and as a world.
We are fragmented. Sometimes we are divided against
ourselves, let alone others, and the result is pain and
sickness.

It can be a therapeutic exercise to gather thoughtfully some fragments of refuse. Let each fragment repre-
sent a part of our lives which has been severed from the
whole. Bless it, and place it where it seems to fit in the
Cross-shaped mosaic. When the mosaic is complete,
bless it as a whole and meditate on the scripture below.

Colossians 2:11–19

Friday: *The Cross*

Jesus, Master Carpenter of Nazareth,
Who won through wood and nails our full salvation
Wield well your tools in this your workshop
That we who come to you rough hewn
May here be fashioned into a truer beauty by your
    hand.

Traditional

*

Week 1: Evening

Holy Christ, you were tested by the evil one
Break in us the hold of power and pride
You knew deep tears and weaknesses
Help us to be vulnerable for you
You followed to the end the Way of the Cross
Help us to be faithful to you to the end of our days.

Psalm 86:1–13
Matthew 5:6–9

Lord, teach us to understand that your Son died to save
us, not from suffering, but from ourselves; not from
injustice, but from being unjust. He died that we might
live as he did, who died to himself.

George MacDonald

God's will would I do
My own will bridle.

God's due would I give
My own due yield.

God's path would I follow
My own path refuse.

Friday: *The Cross*

Christ's death would I ponder
My own death remember.

Christ's agony would I meditate
My love to God make warmer.

Christ's cross would I carry
My own cross forget.

Repentance of sin would I make
Early repentance choose.

The love of Christ would I feel
My own love know.

Carmina Gadelica

*

Week 2: Morning

On this day of Christ's suffering and death
Let us be one with him in his wounds.

Sacred One
Look at our brokenness.
We know that in all creation
Only the human family has strayed from the Sacred
  Way.
Sacred One
Teach us compassion and honour
That we may heal the earth and one another.

Psalm 31
Mark 15:21–32

Christ eternal from the Cross
  bounty bestows from utter loss.
The broken, cold, and stagnant earth

Friday: *The Cross*

awakes with miracles of birth.
And spirits, broken, contrite, cold
   are healed with blessings manifold.
Beauty is free to walk abroad
   and spread the glory of the Lord.

Peter Howard

Saviour, broken on the Cross
Save and raise up those who have none but you to
   turn to:
Those who have suffered loss of work, mobility and
   well-being
Those who are victims of violence, abuse and false
   accusation
Those who are lonely, hungry and homeless.

May the Christ who walks with wounded feet
   walk with us all on the road
May the Christ who serves with wounded hands
   stretch out our hands to serve
May the Christ who loves with the wounded heart
   open our hearts to love.

Anonymous

*

Week 2: Midday reflection at the Shipwrecked Mariners' memorial

In front of the Celtic Cross on the village green is an old wartime naval mine. Painted red and white, it now serves as a collection point for the Shipwrecked Mariners' Society. It states that over one million victims have received welfare, and it concludes with this telling saying: 'There is sorrow on the sea.' On the walls of the former museum beyond it are listed the names of many sailors lost at sea.

In former times, when fierce gales lashed the island, the fishermen used to stand in line holding a rope. The one at the front went into the eye of danger to make safe their storm-tossed boats, secure because of the rope and the strength of his mates who held onto it.

Some islanders serve as honorary coastguards, and several have had boats destroyed by storm. Some have lost a loved one to the sea. At Holy Island funerals the seafarers gather in the fishermen's chapel and sing the hymn below.

Isaiah 43:1–5

Eternal Father, strong to save
whose arm hath bound the restless wave
who bidd'st the mighty ocean deep
its own appointed limits keep:
O hear us when we cry to Thee
for those in peril on the sea.

O Christ, whose voice the waters heard
and hushed their raging at Thy word
who walkedst on the foaming deep
and calm amid the storm didst sleep:
O hear us when we cry to Thee
for those in peril on the sea.

O Holy Spirit who didst brood
upon the waters dark and rude
and bid their angry tumult cease
and give, for wild confusion, peace:
O hear us when we cry to Thee
for those in peril on the sea.

O Trinity of love and power
our brethren shield in danger's hour,

Friday: *The Cross*

from rock and tempest, fire and foe
protect them wheresoe'er they go:
O hear us when we cry to Thee
for those in peril on the sea.

William Whiting[25]

*

Week 2: Evening

Lord Jesus Christ, you gave up everything
   to restore our lost innocence.
You made your home on this earth,
   you overthrew the strongholds of Satan,
   and you freed those in prisons of sin.
Strong yet gentle, you take the burdens
   of all who are broken or bruised.
Suffering and victorious Champion of the poor,
   you open the gates of Heaven's Kingdom
   to all who call upon you.

Psalm 6
Mark 14:32–42

Hail! life-giving Cross
invincible banner of pure religion
gate of paradise
strength of believers
defence of the church.
By you the curse has been undone, destroyed,
the power of death devoured
and we have been raised
from earth to heaven.
Unbeatable weapon
demonic powers' foe
martyrs' glory

boast of holy monks
salvation's harbour,
from you the world receives great mercy.

When all creation saw you,
all things' Maker and Creator,
hang naked on the Cross,
it was changed by fear and wailed.
The sun's light failed and the earth quaked.
The rocks were rent and the temple's veil was torn in
    two.
The dead were raised from their tombs,
and the powers of heaven cried out in astonishment:
How amazing this is!
The Judge is judged,
he wills to suffer death,
to heal and renew the world.

From an Orthodox vespers

*

Week 3: Morning

Holy Jesus, hanged on a tree, victorious over death
Forgive us our sins,
Free us from self-seeking
Power us into new ways.

Psalm 3
Romans 8:33–39

Jesus, Saviour of the world
Come to us in your mercy
We look to you to save and help us.
By your Cross and life laid down you set your people
    free

Friday: *The Cross*

We look to you to save and help us.
When your disciples were about to perish
    you reached down and saved them
We look to you to come to our help.
In the greatness of your mercy, free us from our
    chains
Forgive the sins of all your people.
Come now, and dwell with us, Lord Christ Jesus
Hear our prayer and be with us always
And when you come in your glory
Make us to be one with you
    and to share the life of your kingdom.

From an ancient liturgy

We go in the sign of the Cross of Christ ✢
The Cross before us to keep us true
The Cross behind us to shield us from ill
The Cross above us to lead us through.

*

Week 3: Midday reflection
at Sanctuary Field

Sanctuary Field lies between the priory and the harbour.
A busy pastor visited it twice and had two contrasting
experiences. On his first visit he strode across it quick-
ly, and the sheep on either side scattered. On the second
visit he sat on a bench and quietly meditated. To his
surprise the sheep came to him. There was no threat,
only welcome, in his stillness. That incident changed
the way he related to his human flock when he returned
home. He stopped striding around being over-busy; he

learned to stand back and listen. Souls were drawn to seek his counsel for the first time, for 'deep speaks to deep'.

Jesus likened himself to a shepherd. He predicted that he would be arrested and that his 'sheep', meaning his followers, would be scattered. But he also predicted that when he was 'lifted up' many people would be drawn to him. He was 'lifted up' in two senses: on the wooden cross-beam upon which he died, and after his resurrection, when his human phase was subsumed in his divine role.

The Tree of Death can become the Tree of Life. That was the experience on Lindisfarne. After the Vikings had ransacked the island, faithful monks walked for many miles and years across the land with Cuthbert's coffin. Eventually a new community arose around the shrine of St Cuthbert, and that community restored a daughter community on the island.

Ephesians 2:11–22

I weave a silence onto my lips
I weave a silence into my mind
I weave a silence within my heart
I close my ears to distraction
I close my eyes to attractions
I close my heart to temptations.

David Adam

Lord Jesus
at this hour you hung on the Cross,
stretching out your arms in love to all.
May all the peoples of the world
be drawn to your uplifted love,
especially the people we shall work with next.

Friday: *The Cross*

Lord Jesus
in the midst of mockery and madness
you found peace to remain in your Father's will.
In the midst of the fretful day
Give us peace to remain in our Father's will.

*

Week 3: Evening

O King of the Friday
Whose limbs were stretched on the cross,
O Lord who did suffer
The bruises, the wounds, the loss,
We stretch ourselves beneath the shield of your might;
Some fruit from the tree of your passion
Fall on us this night!

Traditional Irish

Psalm 43
Zechariah 12:10 — 13:1

O Son of God, do a miracle for me and change my heart; your having taken flesh to redeem me was more difficult than to transform my wickedness. It is you who, to help me, went to be scourged by the Jews; you, dear child of Mary, are the refined molten metal of our forge. It is you who made the sun bright, together with the ice; it is you who created the rivers and the salmon all along the river. . . . Though the children of Eve ill deserve the bird flocks and the salmon, it was the Immortal One on the cross who made both salmon and birds.

Fifteenth-century Irish

Friday: *The Cross*

Gather the sufferings of all
Into the communion of the crucified Christ.
Shield and deliver them, good God
Look on them with your merciful gaze.

O Christ who at this evening hour rested in the tomb
And made it become a bed of hope
Visit this house tonight
That we may pass through the death of sleep
And rise from our beds in hope of life eternal.

*

Week 4: Morning

O Christ, you were put to death by cruel people
    who nailed your arms to a cross;
Yet long before you stretched out your arms in love
    to all.
May your way be our way
May we, too, stretch out our arms in love to all.

Psalm 51
John 19:28–37

Imagined reproaches of Christ
O my people, how have I offended you?
Answer me.
I freed you from slavery;
yet you handed me over to death and jeered at me.
O my people.

I opened the sea before you;
You opened my side with a spear!
O my people.

I moved before you in the pillar of cloud;

Friday: *The Cross*

you led me to Pilate!
O my people.

I watched over you in the desert and fed you with
  manna;
you struck me and scourged me!
O my people.

I gave you from the rock living waters of salvation;
you gave me bitter drink, you quenched my thirst
  with vinegar!
O my people.

I struck down kings for you;
you struck me with a reed!
O my people.

I put the sceptre into your hand and made you a
  royal people;
you crowned me with the crown of thorns!
O my people.

I made you great by my boundless power;
you hanged me on the gallows of the cross!
O my people.

Traditional (adapted)

Christ forsaken
Have mercy on all who are forsaken
Christ afraid
Have mercy on all who are afraid
Christ betrayed
Have mercy on all who are betrayed
Christ unnoticed
Have mercy on all who are unnoticed.

*

Week 4: Midday reflection at St Aidan's Church

Andy and Anna Raine are two members of the Northumbria Community who, when they are on the island, say the Community's daily Morning Prayer at St Aidan's Roman Catholic Church. Members of the Community follow a Rule of Life. The twin peaks of this are vulnerability and availability. This is how the Morning Prayer begins:

> One thing have I asked of the Lord,
> This is what I seek:
> That I may dwell in the house of the Lord
> All the days of my life,
> To behold the beauty of the Lord
> And to seek Him in His temple.

A version of the traditional (anonymous) 'St Aidan's Prayer for Holy Island' has been inscribed and displayed in St Aidan's Church:

> Lord, this bare island, make it a place of peace
> Here be the peace of those who do your will
> Here be the peace of brother serving other
> Here be the peace of holy monks obeying
> Here be the peace of praise by dark and day.
> Be this island your Holy Island
> I, Lord, your servant Aidan, make this prayer;
> Be it your care.

Deuteronomy 6:1–9

Call: Who is it that you seek?
Response: We seek the Lord our God.

Friday: *The Cross*

Call: Do you seek Him with all your heart?
Response: Amen. Lord, have mercy.
Call: Do you seek Him with all your soul?
Response: Amen. Lord, have mercy.
Call: Do you seek Him with all your mind?
Response: Amen. Lord, have mercy.
Call: Do you seek Him with all your strength?
Response: Amen. Christ, have mercy.

The Northumbria Community

∗

Week 4: Evening

Sacrificial Love lingers still among us
Calling us to wait and to watch.

Your people praise you at the start of the day
May eating and talking praise you
May thoughts and actions praise you.

Your people praise you at the end of the day
May all the good that has been done praise you
May rest and sleep praise you.

Psalm 116
1 John 1:12–14

Christ of the tears, of the wounds, of the piercings,
May your Cross this night be our shield
Your Cross between us and all enemies without
Your Cross between us and all enemies within
Your Cross our sure way from earth to heaven.

As I enter into sleep
Keep my soul, O Father, keep.
As I enter into rest
Renew my frame, O Saviour blest.

133

Friday: *The Cross*

When I wake with work to do
Holy Spirit, see me through.
Holy Three, my shield, my wall
Be my rest, my joy, my all.

*

Week 5: Morning

You will labour, but God will bless your work.
You will walk, but God will bless your footsteps.
You will suffer, but God will bless your tears.

Jean Vianney

Psalm 142
Song of Songs 8:6–7

Give us sorrow for our violations of human dignity
And our sins against hospitality.
Give us sorrow for our sins
That when our bodies become but ashes
We may live with you for ever.

The outpouring of your love
O crucified One
Wrenches from my heart
Its own outpouring.
Tears of gratitude fill my eyes
Grace of serving fills my being.

*

Week 5: Midday reflection on the safety tower on the causeway

The safety tower by the causeway bridge is provided
for motorists caught by the rising tide. From the top of
the tower one can get an overall view of the shape of the

island. It looks a bit like an axe, with the causeway forming the handle.

Legend says that when Satan raised his giant battle-axe against heaven's gates, God's shaft of lightning struck it from his hand. The flaming axe fell into the North Sea and was changed into the thousand-acre island of Lindisfarne.

This bit of folklore can inspire us to keep Satan's power underfoot, as did the incessant intercessions of people like Cuthbert. What does it mean to do this? To wrestle in our inmost being against our downward tendencies to despise or possess others, to distort truth, to neglect or mistreat creation, including ourselves and our neighbours, to divide ourselves from God and to let complaining replace joy.

As we walk through life, even though the elements rage and events seem to conspire against us, if we keep this symbol of Holy Island in mind we shall be overcomers.

Daniel 10:10–20

Michael the victorious
I do my rounds under thy shield
Conqueror of evil invaders
Cover my back
Ranger of the heavens
Rout out undercover destroyers.

If I travel the world
In the fellowship of Michael's crowd
No harm can befall me anywhere on the globe
'Neath the shelter of thy shield
O Michael the victorious
The jewel of my heart
O Michael the victorious
God's shepherd thou art.

Carmina Gadelica

Friday: *The Cross*

Week 5: Evening

Shadows darken this day
The day Christ was laid in a grave
The darkness shall not engulf us
For with you the darkness is light.

Psalm 77

Just being who you are
not justifying or apologising
it sounds so easy
it's a life work
not to get caught in
producing
performing
proving
keeping accounts of indebtedness
waiting for gratitude, reward
ambition
manipulation
staggering self-pity
but cultivating
the habit of being.

Flannery O'Connor[26]

I make the sign of the Cross of Christ ⁙
My Christ, my Shield, my Saviour;
Each day, each night, in light, in dark,
My Treasure, my dear One,
My eternal home.

Saturday

Sinners and Saints

Cuthbert of Farne

Saturday: *Sinners and Saints*

For many people Saturday is a time for leisure and shopping. These themes colour the first half of the day's prayers. But the week is drawing to a close, and as we prepare to celebrate tomorrow's day of resurrection we move into a higher plane. So thinking about the saints becomes the dominant theme as the day progresses.

Aidan, Cuthbert, Oswald and Columba are the major saints associated with Holy Island, but there are others, including some notable women, whom we think about on the fifth Saturday.

Aidan is 'the people's saint' who brought Christianity to the English-speaking peoples. He died on 31 August 651, but 8 October is believed to be the day when some of his bones were taken from Lindisfarne and eventually to Innis Boffin, Ireland. Other bones were said to be placed in Cuthbert's tomb at Durham. Some people believe that a few of his bones would have been left on his own island of Lindisfarne at the time of the Viking invasion.

Cuthbert was a charismatic evangelist, healer, overseer and contemplative, the first Saxon saint to draw multitudes to him in both life and death.

The boy Oswald fled after his pagan father lost Northumbria's throne and his life. He became a Christian, found sanctuary at Iona, and vowed to evangelize his people if he regained the throne for his family. This he did. From his headquarters at Bamburgh, Oswald invited Iona to send a mission team. The first team failed, but the second, led by Aidan, began the conversion of Northumbria. Oswald gave Aidan land at Lindisfarne, where he established his Christian centre. Oswald translated Aidan's words into the Northumbrian dialect, and made him a welcome guest at the castle.

Columba founded the Iona monastery which trained Oswald and sent Aidan to Lindisfarne. Born into one of the great families of sixth-century northern Ireland, he was a brilliant organizer, poet, song-writer and prophet. Imitating Jesus' lifestyle of love and simplicity, he became the leader of a large network of monasteries and a strategist for the kingdom of God. He appeared in a vision to Oswald in Northumbria, and the monks at Lindisfarne followed his Rule.

Ebbe, Oswald's sister, and Hilda, a more distant relative, both became friends of Aidan and established monasteries. They and a host of other Christians became spiritual mothers and fathers whose wisdom and integrity influenced many people beyond the borders of their own kingdom.

Week 1: Morning

Life-giving God, the world lies open before you
And you summon the day to dawn.
Open our being
And we shall show life.
Open our hearts
And we shall show love.
Open our mouths
And we shall show praise.

Psalm 33
Isaiah 66:7–14a

All that moves on the earth
Bless your God
All that swims in the water
Bless your God
All that flies in the air
Give glory to God who nurtures us all.

Parents and children
Bless your God
Friends and lovers
Bless your God
Musicians and sports-folk
Give glory to God who nurtures us all.

Parks and play areas
Bless your God
Streets and shops
Bless your God
Homes and gardens
Give glory to God who nurtures us all.

Saturday: *Sinners and Saints*

May the raindrops fall lightly on your brow
May the soft winds freshen your spirit
May the sunshine brighten your heart
May the burdens of the day rest lightly upon you
And may God enfold you in love.

*

Week 1: Midday reflection
at Aidan's statue

Aidan has been called the Apostle to the English. He established numerous churches which were like great families. He started the first school for English boys and sent out a stream of missionaries as far south as London. If wealthy people gave him money, he gave it to the poor, or went to the slave market and bought a slave his freedom. Sometimes he even rebuked kings, but his gentleness unlocked the hearts of those he encountered. It still does today.

Recently a man walked around the island with a tape recorder, making up 'rap' poems inspired by Aidan. One of them went something like this:

Oh Aidan was an Irish lad who found the light of God.
He saw it in the sunshine, he saw it in each sod.
It brought him to Iona, the place that's thin with sin,
It led him on to Lindisfarne a mighty work to begin.
To everyone he met he said, 'Hi there, how good to see
That Christ is in the eye of you and you and me.

Saturday: *Sinners and Saints*

Would you care to know some more, of this guy who
   lights our earth?
In his name maybe I can help you, at your work or at
   your hearth?'
The people flocked around him, for he walked without a horse.
They flocked around this friend who gave his goods
   to every sort.
Was there ever such a gentle man who prophesied
   and prayed,
Who with a rough, rude people stayed and stayed
   and stayed
Till light streamed north and south through people
   he had trained?
And when Aidan went to heaven the light with us
   remained.
So bless the Lord for this gentle soul and the light
   that won't go out.
Come on, me lads, get off your horse; tell the folk
   what it's all about.

Isaiah 6:1–8

Lord Jesus, simplicity and a deep love for people
shone out of your apostle Aidan.
Grant that, like him, we may be gentle in our loving
and bold in our speaking
that we might inspire others to learn your ways,
and so pass on the fire of faith.

*

Week 1: Evening

Calm me, O Lord, as you stilled the storm
Still me, O Lord, keep me from harm
Let all the tumult within me cease
Enfold me, Lord, in your peace.

David Adam

Psalm 92
Luke 10:21–24

Sent from Iona with blessings in his hand
He arrived in Northumbria, a stranger in the land.
Gentle in his words and humble in attire
he talked to the people of a Presence divine.

Leaving far behind all worldly goods on high
He walked among the people with nothing left to hide
As grains in the sand and poor in heart and soul
The power of the Gospel, the Word to make them Whole.

Andrew Lobb[27]

The day's toil is done
The birds cease their songs
We rest our frames.

May the God of gentleness
be with you, caressing you
with sunlight and rain and wind.
May his tenderness

shine through you to warm all those
who are hurt and lonely.
May the blessing of gentleness
be upon you.

*

Week 2: Morning

Holy God of Cuthbert and the saints
Go before us now.
God of the hills, God of the outposts
Go before us now.
God of the streets, God of the people
Go before us now.

Psalm 121
2 Corinthians 6:3–13

Make whole the leisure and activity of this day
Restrain its hostile impulses
Fill its moments.

The boy Cuthbert early sensed your call; may children in our land be introduced to your Holy Spirit, be attracted by holy lives, and respond to divine callings.

The sport-loving Cuthbert became an athlete of the Spirit; may sports people see their training as a step towards the eternal race.

Cuthbert shared his faith with people far from reach; may church people reach out to the unchurched with compassion.

Cuthbert warned against schism and carefully

guarded unity; may envy be banished and may communion be restored in the church.

> May the saints and the Saviour watch over us
> And keep us true in all we do.
> May we live the rest of this day
> In the joy of the Saviour's will.

*

Week 2: Midday reflection at the Cuthbert of Farne sculpture in the priory grounds

The priory ruins, which are managed by English Heritage, are those of the small Benedictine daughter house of the much larger St Cuthbert's Community at Durham, built in the twelfth century. Although there are now no traces of the original Celtic priory, we know that St Cuthbert, who was prior here between 664 and 676, used to shed tears from the depths of his heart as he celebrated Holy Communion in the stone church which was probably on this site. And after the existing priory was built the monks had a vision of Cuthbert, who came out of the parish church into the priory where he celebrated Holy Communion. During the Second World War Durham people saw visions of Cuthbert protecting the city from attacking aircraft.

In 2001 Lawson Fenwick's great sculpture of Cuthbert of Farne was installed in the priory grounds. It is good to linger in its compassionate ambience and recall a story of Cuthbert, such as the following.

Cuthbert was making his way southward along the

146

river Teviot, teaching and baptizing the country folk, and taking with him a boy he was training.

'Do you think someone has prepared your midday meal today?' he asked the boy.

'I have no family or friends in this district,' the boy replied, and he clearly did not expect unknown strangers to provide for their needs.

'Cheer up, the Lord will provide for those who trust him,' Cuthbert assured him, quoting Jesus' words, 'Seek first the kingdom of God and all these other things shall be given to you.'

After building up the boy's faith by quoting such scriptures, Cuthbert saw an eagle flying overhead and said to the boy: 'This is the eagle the Lord has instructed to provide us with food today.'

Shortly after, as they continued to walk, they saw the eagle settle on the riverbank. At Cuthbert's direction the boy ran to it and saw a large fish in its mouth, which he brought to Cuthbert.

'Why didn't you give our fisherman his half of it, since he was denying himself?' said Cuthbert.

So the boy gave half to the eagle. They boiled the other half in the company of some local folk, with whom they shared it, worshipping the Lord and giving thanks. Then they set out to the mountains, led by God, to teach and baptize the people.[28]

1 Samuel 3:1–11

Heavenly Father
grant me grace to fulfil my calling
by following your way of incarnate love
that I might make you known
to those I seek to serve in your name.

Saturday: *Sinners and Saints*

Take me, break me, give me
that I might tell others of the journey
and share with them your food for the way
so that they will come to you
and we will live
for ever.

Andrew Clitherow

*

Week 2: Evening

Holy God
you called Cuthbert out of the darkness of night
    to be the Fire of the North.
Kindle in us the fire of your love
That we, with your saints, may blaze for you for
    ever.

Psalm 119:49–64
Ezekiel 34:11–16

My heart's desire is to serve the King
    To heed his call in everything.
My heart's desire is to touch his cloak
    To release his power in ordinary folk.
My heart's desire is to pray like flint
    Till demons flee and winds relent.
My heart's desire is that sick are cured
    And that hostile mockers praise the Lord.
My heart's desire is that Christians are one
    In a church in peace and communion.

Saturday: *Sinners and Saints*

My heart's desire is to reach the throne
Where God reigns in glory with his own.

Cuthbert's Prayer the Community of
Aidan and Hilda

Heavenly Father, who called Cuthbert from tending sheep to be a shepherd of the people; help us, inspired by his example, to heal the sick, to guard unity, to storm heaven's gates, and to bring those who are lost home to your fold.

Now, robed in stillness, in this quiet place, emptied of all I was, I bring all that I am, your gift of shepherding to use and bless.[29]

*

Week 3: Morning

High King of heaven, who raised up Oswald to plant the healing tree of Christ's passion in his kingdom, redeem our land from the curse of disobedience and bring it under your just and gentle rule, through Jesus Christ our Lord.

Psalm 72
Deuteronomy 17:14–19

If our mouths were full of song as the sea
Our tongues with joyful sounds like the roar of its
   waves
Our lips with praise like the outspread sky
We still could not thank you enough, Lord,
For the good you have done to us and our forebears.

Saturday: *Sinners and Saints*

If our eyes were shining like the sun and the moon
Our hands stretched out like eagles' wings in the air
Our feet as swift as the wild deer
We still could not thank you enough, Lord,
For the good you have done to us and our forebears.

You rescued us from the tyrant
You freed us from slavery
In times of famine you fed us
In times of plenty you built us up
From violence you delivered us
From plagues you saved us
Therefore to you who breathed life into us
We shall give praise with all our breath
Honour with all our memory
Worship with all our being.

Traditional Jewish liturgy (adapted)

In our pleasures
Your kingdom come
In our leaders
Your kingdom come
In our gatherings
Your kingdom come
On the roads
Your kingdom come
On the networks
Your kingdom come
In each thing we do this day
Your kingdom come

May we do this day on earth
As the saints do in heaven.

*

Week 3: Midday reflection facing Bamburgh

After seventeen years at Iona, Oswald learned that his uncle, Northumbria's King Edwin, had been killed and his kingdom was being desecrated by a pagan tyrant who killed Oswald's brother. Oswald collected a small army to confront the invader near Hadrian's Wall, and the night before the battle he erected a wooden cross in the ground to show that he would fight, and intended to reign, as a Christian. There he knelt with his soldiers and prayed to God for victory, 'for he knows we have undertaken a just war for the safety of our nation.' Columba appeared to him in a dream and promised him victory, because his cause was just. The place of victory, still marked by a cross, is known as Heavenfield to this day.

Oswald gave Aidan every possible assistance in his mission, rose early to pray with his hands open to heaven, and became a role model throughout Europe for a just and Christian ruler. According to Northumberland County Council, who have adopted it as their own, St Oswald's was the first English flag.

Joshua 1:1–9

We draw aside in the midst of the day
We weep for the hungry and poor
The children mistreated, those broken by force
And the maimed who can't finish their course.

We plead for your justice to fill all the lands
As the waters cover the sands.

Saturday: *Sinners and Saints*

We pray against cruelty, hatred and pain
Pride and greed for gain
We pray for the homeless and victims of war
The strangers to love at the door.

We plead for your justice to fill all the lands
As the waters cover the sands.

Andrew Dick

*

Week 3: Evening

Glory to the High King
Glory to the Son
Glory to the Spirit
Ever Three in One.

Psalm 61
2 Chronicles 7:11–27

Oswald used his wealth and position to serve the common good. He died fighting valiantly in a just defence of his kingdom, praying that God would save the souls of those who were dying around him.

My God, save the souls of those who destroy their
enemies
My God, save the souls of those who destroy
reputations
My God, save the souls of those who destroy the
unborn
My God, save the souls of the victims one and all.

Saturday: *Sinners and Saints*

High King of heaven and earth
from whom all authority flows
may the diverse authorities of our times
acknowledge you as the Source of life
emulate you as the Servant King
and fear you as the Judge of truth.

May heaven's King go with us
May Christ's Cross grow in us
May the Spirit's fire glow in us
Till the final victory dawns.

*

Week 4: Morning

Let me bless almighty God,
whose power extends over sea and land
and whose angels watch over all.
Let me study sacred books to calm my soul.
I pray for peace, kneeling at heaven's gates.
Let me do my daily work, gathering seaweed,
catching fish, giving food to the poor.
Let me say my daily prayers, sometimes chanting,
sometimes quiet, always thanking God.
Delightful it is to live on a peaceful isle, in a quiet cell,
serving the King of kings.

Attributed to Columba

Lord, my circumstances are so different,
    yet your power extends to where I am.
Your angels watch over me.
Fill my mind; grant me peace.

Help me do my daily work, to say my prayers,
    whether in bustle or stillness.
May it be my delight to serve you as King of this day.

Psalm 34:1–14
Lamentations 3:19–33

Columba turned his back on his beloved Ireland to show that he repented for his part in the violence in that land, and to win as many converts to Christ's kingdom in a new land as had perished in war in his own. He wrote: 'How swift is the speed of my coracle, its stern turned to Derry. I grieve at the errand o'er the noble sea, travelling to Alba of the ravens, my foot in my good little coracle, my sad heart still bleeding. . . .' In the spirit of Columba we pray:

I turn my back, Lord, on ill-will, envy, hate;
I leave behind regrets and bitter traits.
I turn my back, Lord, on possessiveness and greed;
I leave behind my headstrong foolish ways.
I turn my back, Lord, on misuse of earth and souls;
I leave behind my heedless, selfish days.

May we grow, little by little, day by day, in goodness and greatness of spirit. May wisdom, discernment and eloquence increase in us that we may serve our communities well.[30]

Dearest Lord, be
A bright flame before us
A guiding star above us
A smooth path beneath us
A kindly shepherd behind us.

*

Week 4: Midday reflection
by St Coombs Farm

Holy Island has two farms, one of which is named St Coombs, after St Columba, founder of the Iona monastery, from which Aidan came. There is a certain appropriateness to this, since Columba loved animals. His favourite bird was the heron.

Columba wrote a Rule for his monks, and Aidan later instituted it in the first monastery on Lindisfarne. A Rule set out goals and values by which a group of monks pledged to live. People who were not monks but wished to be involved in the monastic community would also adopt some of these, working out which ones were practical for them with a spiritual guide, whom they called an *anam cara* or 'soul friend'.

A growing number of people today, including some Holy Island residents, do something similar. Although Columba's original Rule is lost, an eighth-century Rule attributed to him may well reflect something of the original. It includes values such as these:

Three labours in the day – prayers, work and reading.
Forgiveness from the heart for everyone.
Constant prayers for those who trouble you.

1 Corinthians 14:1–12

That I might see the ocean's heaving waves
    chanting music to their Father,
That contrition might come upon my heart,

Saturday: *Sinners and Saints*

That I might bless the Lord who conserves all Heaven
  with its countless bright orders,
Land, strand and flood.
That I might search books that are good for my soul,
At times kneeling to beloved Heaven
  and at times singing psalms,
At times serving the poor and at times contemplating
  the King of Heaven, the Holy One.

Columba

*

Week 4: Evening

Let us go for a while to the courts of heaven
Let us join with the saints in praise.

O God, you are the Father of all who have believed:
From whom all hosts of angels have life and power
  received.
O God, you are the Maker of all created things:
The righteous Judge of judges, almighty King of
  kings.

Columba

Psalm 119:1–16
Joel 2:28–32a

On that night when St Columba, by a happy and
blessed death passed from earth to heaven, while I and
others with me were fishing in the valley of the river
Find, we saw the whole vault of heaven become sud-
denly illuminated. Towards the east there appeared

Saturday: *Sinners and Saints*

something like an immense pillar of fire, which seemed to illuminate the whole earth like the summer sun at noon. After that the column penetrated the heavens, darkness followed, as if the sun had just set.

Adamnan

God of the call, we pray for those
   who feel thwarted in their vocation;
May they do on earth as the saints do in heaven.

God from whom all truth and justice flow,
We pray for the rule of law to prevail;
May we do on earth as the saints do in heaven.

God of resurrection, in their worship
   may our churches bring glory to you,
May they bring hope and friendship to the people,
May they do on earth as the saints do in heaven.

Kindle in us, O God, the flame of that love which never ceases, that it may burn in us, giving light to others. May that light which shone so brightly in Columba, take away the darkness of our hearts, and bring us to share with him the light of the eternal dwelling.

The peace of Columba be ours
   in the smooth and in the rough.
The peace of Columba be ours
   in our sleeping and rising.

*

Week 5: Morning

Most glorious Giver of Life
May coasts and islands praise you
May town and country praise you
May healers and artists praise you.
Darkness and light praise you
Stars and moon praise you
The guillemots and the gulls praise you
The ducks and the sea otters praise you
The Gospels and the relics praise you
Cuthbert, Aidan and the risen ones of Lindisfarne
    praise you.
May all creation praise you and give you glory for
    ever.

Psalm 18:1–19
Luke 14:7–11

Grant, O Lord, that your church in this land
may be true to its birthright.
Kindle in us the adventure of obedience, the single
    eye,
the humble and generous heart,
which marked Aidan and your Celtic saints.

Faithful God, from the first-fruits of the English people
who turned to Christ, you called Ebbe, Chad,
Cuthbert, Hilda and many others to holy learning and
high service. May we learn from them to pattern the
ways of Christ in our time.

Saturday: *Sinners and Saints*

God of Life,
Thank you for those who have
   upheld noble values
   exercised good judgement
   guided the uncertain
   excited others to live holy lives.
Impart to us wisdom to understand your ways
Help us to manage well the tasks of this day
Make us co-creators with you
That when day fades we may come to you without
   shame.

*

Week 5: Midday reflection
at the war memorial

Human beings have a deep need to identify and acknowledge exceptional skill, daring, flair or goodness. Paul of Tarsus encouraged Christians to live energetically for God and people, constantly aware of the 'great cloud of witnesses' who had lived this way and who were still alive and present (Hebrews 11).

In the days of Aidan and Cuthbert a Christian who had influenced many others to live holy lives was declared to be a saint without more ado at his or her funeral. It was soon realized that there is great value in sometimes celebrating the whole community of these holy people, including those about whom not enough is known to allocate a particular day to them. The Book of Wisdom says that such people shine for ever like sparks in a field of stubble.

As a result of such reflection, another truth dawned:

Saturday: *Sinners and Saints*

every human life is precious, and should be treated with a sense of wonder. Thus Christians delight in remembering and treasuring all souls: loved ones they have known, and more distant forebears; those in one's neighbourhood who have passed away, and those who have perished in war.

The flowers that beautify St Mary's Church week by week, and the hymn and prayer books and kneelers, are mostly donated in memory of someone who has passed away. The annual Remembrance service at the war memorial is an important event in Holy Island's yearly calendar.

Holy Island remembers its dead well, and so should we.

1 Corinthians 15:42–49

Since it was you, O Christ, who bought each soul –
At the time it gave up its life
At the time of returning to clay
At the time of the shedding of blood
At the time of severing the breath
At the time you delivered judgement –
May your peace be on your ingathering of souls
Jesus Christ, Son of gentle Mary
Your peace be upon your own ingathering.

Carmina Gadelica

*

Week 5: Evening

Eternal Creator of the weeks and years
As this week draws to a close, draw close to us
And we will draw close to you.

Eternal Creator of the days and nights
As darkness deepens, draw near to us
And we will draw near to you.

Psalm 110
Wisdom 3:1–9

Eternal Wisdom,
Come into the storehouse of our memories
Be present through the silent hours
And bring us to your glorious light.

May we, like Patrick, surmount all kinds of trials
    in our zeal that people come to know you.
May we, like Brigid, flow in generous creativity
    in our hospitality towards others.
May we, like Columba, leave behind comforts we
    hold dear
    in order to bring life where there was death.
May we, like Oswald and Ebbe, heal and serve our
    land
    with compassion and valour.
May we like, Aidan, offer the gentle understanding
    of Christ
    to everyone we meet.
May we, like Chad and his brothers, show that a true
    leader
    is a true servant.

161

Saturday: *Sinners and Saints*

May we, like Hilda, bring out the best in others
    and delight to see them grow.
May we, like Cuthbert, storm the gates of heaven
    until the kingdoms
    of this world become the kingdom of our God.
Jesus, master of apostles, teacher of evangelists,
    strength of martyrs,
    friend of the poor, crown of saints,
    lead us through the night into a day of renewal.
May we be counted among your saints
    and shine in your presence for ever.

May you be an island in the sea
A hill in the valley
A light in the dark.

About the Community of Aidan and Hilda

The Community of Aidan and Hilda is a dispersed body of Christians who seek to cradle a Christian spirituality for today, renew the church and heal the land. It welcomes people in all churches and countries who wish to be wholly available to the Holy Trinity, and to the way of Jesus as revealed to us in the Bible.

In the earthing of that commitment members of the Community draw inspiration from Celtic saints such as Aidan and Hilda. Aidan, the people's saint, who brought Christianity to English speakers through love, not fear. Hilda, pioneer of women's ministry, trainer of evangelists, encourager of overlooked folk, mother of the church. Together they are a sign of soul friends of different race and gender working together for the common good.

Members follow a Way of Life, with a soul friend, based on prayer, study, simplicity, care for the creation and mission. They seek to renew the church by weaving together the separated Catholic, Reformed, Orthodox and Pentecostal strands, and by fostering a new kind of monasticism.

The Community began in 1994 and has members on four continents, including a USA Order. Its Guardian, Revd Ray Simpson, leads its operational group and gives account to trustees. It has Advisors from different church streams, and the Community Soul Friend is Bishop Ian Harland.

About the Community of Aidan and Hilda

It welcomes Friends, who subscribe to its quarterly magazine, *The Aidan Way*. It sponsors workshops, study programmes, personal and private retreats, and publishes, through the St Aidan Press, experimental study and worship resources for individuals and churches.

St Chad's House at Leek in Staffordshire is staffed by Community members and welcomes guests for retreats or healing ministry. The Community's main office, retreat and guest house is The Open Gate, Holy Island, Berwick upon Tweed, TD15 2SD. Tel: (01289) 389222. Fax: (01289) 389378. Email: community@theopengate. ndo.co.uk. Non-residents are welcome to Night Prayer every week-night.

For a Resources Catalogue, information about public and private retreats or for the Introductory Pack (£1.50 payable to 'St Aidan Press') write to the office. Website: http://www.aidan.org.uk.

Notes

1. Old Barbara Macphie told this to Alexander Carmichael.
2. Ian Fosten is the first Director of the St Cuthbert's Centre (opened in 1999).
3. Based on *St Patrick's Breastplate*.
4. © L. Smith and the Dean and Chapter of Durham Cathedral.
5. John Scotus Eriugena, *Perriphyseon: The Division of Nature* (Bellarmin, 1987).
6. In Traherne, *Poems, Centuries and Three Thanksgivings* (Oxford University Press, 1966).
7. Echoes a prayer said on Christmas Eve at Bethlehem by Archbishop George Appleton.
8. From *Against the Heresies*.
9. A prophecy received by Myrtle Kerr of Rostrevor Christian Renewal Centre, Northern Ireland.
10. Based on 'Blessings from Rock Community Church', Dunbarton, 2000.
11. From Pelagius' letter to an elderly friend.
12. From *How the Irish Saved Civilisation* (Doubleday, 1995).
13. From St Patrick's Declaration in *Saint Patrick's World* ed. Liam de Paor (Four Courts Press, 1993).
14. Ascribed to Rabanus Maurus, a sixth-century solitary in Gaul.
15. From *St Patrick's Declaration*.
16. From Columbanus' letter to Pope Boniface IV.
17. Sometimes attributed to Brigid.

18. From Bede's *Life of Cuthbert* in *The Age of Bede*, trans. J.F. Webb (Penguin, 1985).
19. From the Christian Meditation Centre, Dunlaoguire, Ireland.
20. A mentally handicapped Scotsman, who up to the day of his death had never uttered a rational word, opened his eyes in amazement at what was revealed to his soul by the Spirit of God, and spoke these words in his dying hour.
21. c. AD 735–804.
22. From *The Mountain Behind the Mountain* (T.&T. Clark, 1993).
23. c. AD 200.
24. From the Book of Remembrance, Cathedral of St Paul the Apostle, Los Angeles, California.
25. William Whiting, died 1878.
26. From *The Habit of Being: The Letters of Flannery O'Connor* (Farrat Straus Giroux, 1979).
27. © Andrew Lobb, August 2001. To be used only with permission from Swarland Sound, 2 The Square, Swarland, Northumberland, NE65 9JQ. Email: andrewlobb@bigfoot.com.
28. From information recorded by an anonymous monk of Lindisfarne.
29. From Cuthbert's Prayer, St Aidan's Chapel, Bradford Cathedral.
30. Reflects Columba's prayer for a boy.

Acknowledgements

I am grateful for permission to quote from the following works:

'Ebb tide', 'I weave a silence' and 'Calm me, O Lord' from David Adam, *The Edge of Glory* (SPCK, 1985).

'When my life seems all duty and dust' and 'We draw aside in the midst of the day' by Andrew Dick.

'Sent from Iona with blessings in his hand . . .' Words of a song, © Andrew Lobb, August 2001. To be used only with permission from Swarland Sound, 2 The Square, Swarland, Northumberland, NE65 9JQ. Email: andrewlobb@bigfoot.com.

'One thing have I asked of the Lord' and 'Who is it that you seek?' are part of Northumbria Community's Daily Office from *Celtic Daily Prayer*, published in the UK by HarperCollins (2001) and the USA by HarperSanFrancisco (2001).

'When the last storm has abated', © L. Smith and the Dean and Chapter of Durham Cathedral.

'Walking along a cliff-top' from Martin Wallace, *Reflections* (Tiley Prints booklet).

All extracts attributed to the Community of Aidan and Hilda are © St Aidan Press, 1995.

Other books on Celtic Spirituality available from the Canterbury Press

CELTIC BENEDICTION *Morning and Night Prayer*
J PHILIP NEWELL, design and calligraphy by Vera Brice
A beautifully illustrated daily prayer book, with original morning and evening prayers in the Celtic tradition.
1-85311-337-9 • 128pp • 198×126mm • **hardback colour illustrated** • **£9.99**

CELTIC BLESSINGS *Making all things sacred*
BRENDAN O'MALLEY, calligraphy by Shirley Norman
Blessing prayers for dedicating everyday activities and objects.
1-85311-199-6 • 224pp • 197×126mm • **paperback** • £7.99

GOD AT EVERY GATE *Prayers and blessings for pilgrims*
BRENDAN O'MALLEY
Celtic prayers which take their inspiration from the sights and sounds of creation.
1-85311-162-7 • 192pp • 180×105mm • **paperback** • £5.99

AN IONA PRAYER BOOK
PETER MILLAR
A bestselling prayer book that follows the pattern of daily worship in Iona Abbey.
1-85311-205-4 • 128pp • 178×111mm • **paperback** • £5.99

For a catalogue of our publications or to place an order, call our Customer Services on 01603 - 612914 or visit our website: www.scm-canterburypress.co.uk

LaVergne, TN USA
27 September 2010
198647LV00007B/36/P